The De...

The Story ...

Melvin Ridgway

The "Desford" Trainer A complete flying trainer embodying
all essentials to cover the whole of "ab initio" and "intermediate" stages of flying training

REID & SIGRIST

Contents

Acknowledgments

Leicestershire County Council—Alison Clague

Roy Bonser

Windmill Aviation

Victoria Miles

Abbie Ridgway

Kathleen Ridgway

Ken Ellis

Introduction

Being an aviation enthusiast and working for Caterpillar at the former Desford Aerodrome site I thought I would attempt to research the story of the Desford Trainer and the work of Reid and Sigrist. I would often be asked, as fellow employees knew that I was interested in aircraft, about the Desford Trainer. Having obtained an old copy of Flight Magazine at the Farnborough airshow in the 1970's, showing an illustration of the 'Desford' trainer on the front cover (see front cover of this book), I knew that Reid and Sigrist had built a number of aircraft nearby at Desford Aerodrome. After reading *Roy Bonsers' superb book called Aviation In Leicestershire and Rutland, which included information about Desford Aerodrome and the Desford trainer, I began to compile information about Reid and Sigrist and the Desford Trainer. I visited Snibson discovery park in 2013, to view the disassembled 'Desford' after the aircraft was given to Leicestershire County Council from it's previous owners, the Strathallan collection, based in Scotland. I was sad to see it in pieces but then in 2014, Leicestershire County Council decided to restore the aircraft, using the skills of Carl Tyers at Windmill Aviation, based in Northamptonshire. During the period leading up to the 100th Anniversary of the formation of the Royal Air Force (RAF), a number of Caterpillar employees and Desford In Bloom also decided to construct a statue of the Desford which is displayed outside of the main gate at the Caterpillar site.

Research for the book started around this time as a number of questions were raised about the aircraft, including, was the aircraft operated by the RAF? Why was only one built? Etc. Research for the book consisted of National Archive searches, the Civil Aviation Authority (CAA) website, internet searches, visits to the Leicestershire County Council museum archive and general background reading. The book looks at the history of Reid and Sigrist, including their first attempt at building an aircraft, the Snargasher, followed by the Desford trainer and its subsequent conversion by the British Government into a research aircraft to investigate prone pilot positions for future aircraft designs. Due to a larger amount of information being available for the subsequent conversion of the 'Desford' into the 'Bobsleigh', much of the technical section of the book is based on the 'Bobsleigh Conversion'

* Roy Bonser sadly passed away in December 2020 at the age of 91, during the Second World War he worked at the Desford aerodrome site overhauling and repairing Boulton Paul Fighters.

Chapter One
Reid & Sigrist

Reid and Sigrist (R&S) was formed in 1927 by Sqn Ldr George Reid DFC and Frederick Sigrist. Sqn Ldr George Reid DFC served with the Royal Naval Air Service in the First World War and then stayed on with the RAF, retiring in 1926. He designed a range of aircraft instruments including a blind flying panel for the Hawker Tomtit trainer. The blind flying panel could be used to simulate flying in cloud or at night using the aircrafts instruments for reference.

Frederick Sigrist also know as 'uncle Fred' started his career as a garage mechanic in Southampton, he then started working for Sopwith's in 1911 as an engineer on their Schooner Neva. He then moved into the world of aircraft design, producing a number of aircraft layouts for Sopwith which were then turned into blueprints. In a retirement tribute to him in 1940 Flight magazine noted: "In the early days Sigrist had an uncanny knack of producing the best results from primitive materials... He possessed great executive and organising ability and, like [Thomas] Sopwith, had the happy ability of picking the right men and getting the best out of them." Fred Sigrist finally became chief engineer at Sopwith, designing aircraft and managing the production of aircraft for use in the First World War. At the end of the First World War he took semi-retirement but returned when Sopwith went into liquidation and was reformed as H.G. Hawker Engineering. Fred Sigrist became a Millionaire and used some of his wealth to invest in Sqn Ldr George Reid's aircraft instrument business. The new company acquired the rights to the designs of Reid's previous company, Reid Manufacturing & Construction Company Ltd, which had designed and made precision aircraft instrumentation, most notably an aircraft turn and slip indicator, that Reid had invented and developed, and a pilot testing apparatus. Fred Sigrist suffered from ill health and retired in 1940, moving to the Bahamas, to seek a better climate. He died in Nassau on 10th December 1956, age 72.

A picture of Frederick Sigrist (1884-1956) seen in the cockpit of an aircraft possibly a Sopwith aircraft.

In December 1935 R&S expanded its business into contract management for the Air Ministry, opening 7 Elementary and Reserve Flying Training School (E&RFTS, later 7 EFTS) at Desford, Leicestershire, in December 1935. This was followed in 1938 by two more E&RFTSs, 21 at Stapleford Tawney, Essex, and 28 at Meir, Staffordshire.

Further diversification followed in 1937 when R&S opened an aircraft design department, their experience in pilot training led them to design an aircraft that they thought may meet the needs of the RAF as a training aircraft. This aircraft was called the Reid & Sigrist RS.1 Trainer

- After the Second World War Reid & Sigrist was requested by the British Government to produce cameras based on the Leica patents and drawings which had been seized by the allies. Cameras were produced from 1951 until 1964. The company ceased to exist as a separate entity when it was bought by the Decca Record Company at the end of 1954.

Chapter One
Reid & Sigrist

Advertisements the 1930's and 40's showing the range of equipment and services offered

by Reid & Sigrist

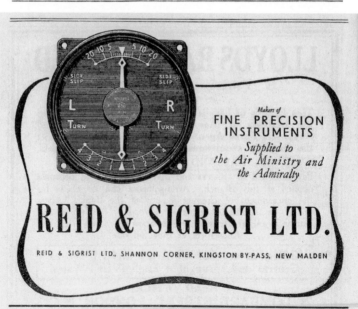

Chapter One
Reid & Sigrist

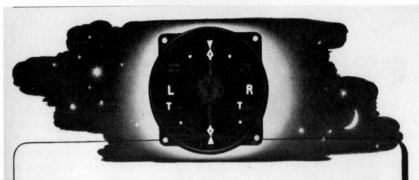

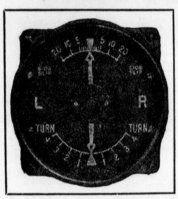
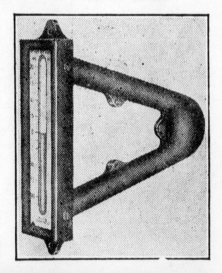

Chapter One
Reid & Sigrist

Chapter One
Reid & Sigrist Snargasher

Reid & Sigrist's (R&S) first venture into aircraft construction began during 1938-39 when the RS.1 Trainer was designed at the company's main works at Shannon Corner, New Malden, Surrey and built close by. When completed, the aircraft was taken to Desford for final assembly and flight trials where, at an early stage, workers jokingly called it the 'Snargasher'. Although it had no specific meaning the nickname stuck and became a popular name for the aircraft.

The RS.1 Trainer was a three-seat tandem trainer of plywood-covered wooden construction with a fixed cantilever undercarriage. In the design stage specific attention was given to possible mass production. With this in mind, specialized knowledge from experts in the automotive industry was sought.

Powered by two 205hp de Havilland Gipsy Six II inverted air-cooled engines driving de Havilland two position controllable screws, it was primarily intended to serve as an advanced trainer for the conversion of pilots from single to twin-engine aircraft. The design also made provision for the teaching of navigation, bombing, wireless operation and gunnery. Under the continuous canopy the pupil sat forward, the instructor or observer immediately behind, with the radio operator or gunner aft. The rear end of the canopy was fitted with a tip up cowl underneath which was a special R5 mounting for a Lewis gun. The mounting enabled the gun to be traversed through 180 degrees and have 90 degrees of elevation and could be fired almost vertically over the sides. For use in the bombing role, a prone aiming position was provided in the belly beneath the two cockpits.

Flown for the first time early in 1939 by George Edward Lowdell and registered G-AEOD (constructor number 1) it made its public debut at the Royal Aeronautical Society's Garden Party at Heathrow on 14th May, receiving its certificate of airworthiness shortly afterwards on 3rd June. The RS.1 was given extensive tests and trials, including a series witnessed by representatives of the Royal Aircraft Establishment (RAE) at Farnborough, Hampshire. Throughout the test period the aircraft performed well and was a pleasant aircraft to fly. It was not accepted by the RAF as no requirement existed for an aircraft of this category at the time.

G-AEOD during a very low fly-by during a demonstration at Desford. The attractive lines of the aircraft are evident

Chapter One
Reid & Sigrist Snargasher

The RS.1 G-AEOD appeared next to a specially modified Spitfire at the Brussels International Salon in July 1939 (also see picture on page 23)

Speed Spitfire (Type 323)

In November 1937 a modified Messerschmitt Bf 109 V13 (D-IPKY), raised the world landplane speed record to 379 mph (610 km/h). Previously it had been held by Howard Hughes flying a Hughes H-1 racing aircraft at 352 mph (566 km/h).

Funded by the British Air Ministry in 1938 the 48th production Spitfire Mk I (K9834) was taken from the line and significantly modified as a one off for an attempt on this record.

All military equipment was removed, the wings were shortened and rounded tips fitted.

A 4 blade wooden propeller was fitted to a specially modified Rolls Royce Merlin II engine which utilising a "racing fuel" of petrol, methanol and benzol produced 2,100 hp (1,565 kW).

Further streamlining included introduction of a tailskid and a racing windscreen. The panel lines were smoothed and flush rivets replaced the round head rivets.

Finally a highly polished royal blue paint scheme with a silver flash was adopted with the distinctive designation N-17 issued.

Reid & Sigrist Snargasher

G-AEOD shows off the tapered elliptical wing plan in the above view. The rear cockpit gun position can also be seen although the aircraft was not armed at this time. The style of registration lettering makes the last two letters difficult to distinguish from one another (Flight via JM Collection)

Rear end view and head on view of the RS.1 Snargasher. The division between flaps and ailerons can be seen, and from the rear the walkway on the port wing for access to the cockpits. (Flight via JM Collection)

The Scale which is provided by the pilot shows the aircraft to be surprisingly small, being just a little larger than a post-war Gemini twin although it was significantly heavier and also faster (Flight via JM Collection)

Reid & Sigrist Snargasher

(Above View) A side view of the 'Snargasher' showing the large canopy and (below view) flying low and fast over an aerodrome, possibly Desford.

Reid & Sigrist Snargasher

Close up view of the front of the RS.1 shows the landing light in the nose and below the pitot mast. The Gipsy Six II engines were fitted with de Havilland variable pitch propellers with a clearance of less than a foot between the propeller arc and the fuselage (Ken Ellis)

G-AEOD continued to wear its civil registration during the war, combined with RAF camouflage, when used by 7 EFTS and by Reid and Sigrst as a communications aircraft. In this view the rear cockpit cover appears to have been removed (Flight via JM Collection)

Reid & Sigrist Snargasher

The RS.1 preparing to land with flaps deployed, wearing the wartime camouflage and civil registration (Flight via JM Collection)

Mocked-up illustration of the RS.1 in an RAF training scheme, one of several produced by the company (Flight via JM Collection)

Reid & Sigrist Snargasher

The Snargasher makes a very low pass over the main building at Desford (Ken Ellis)

Reid & Sigrist Snargasher

A Reid & Sigrist Christmas card depicting a flypast by the Snargasher (Ken Ellis)

(Left) Pilot G.E. Lowdell standing in the cockpit of the Snargasher (Ken Ellis)

Reid & Sigrist Snargasher

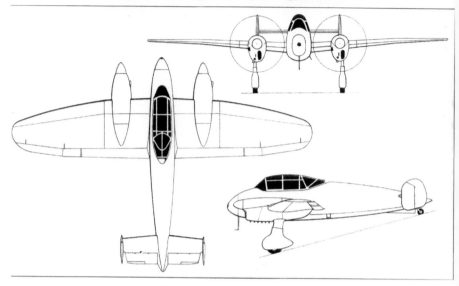

Plan views of the Snargasher

A picture of the Snargasher attending the 1938 Heathrow Royal Aeronautical Society Garden Party (Photo Joe Connolly)

Reid & Sigrist Snargasher

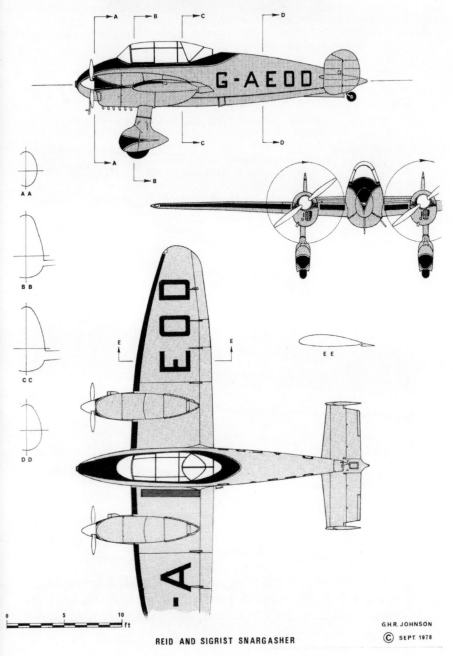

G-AEOD

REID AND SIGRIST SNARGASHER

G.H.R. JOHNSON
Ⓒ SEPT 1978

Reid & Sigrist Snargasher

Reid and Sigrist adverts appeared in the aviation press in the mid-1940. It shows two proposed versions, assumed to be the RS.2 (a proposed development of the Snargasher), both with retractable undercarriage for use as a fighter or bomber trainer. Engines were quoted as being of 240/260hp with a top speed of 230mph.

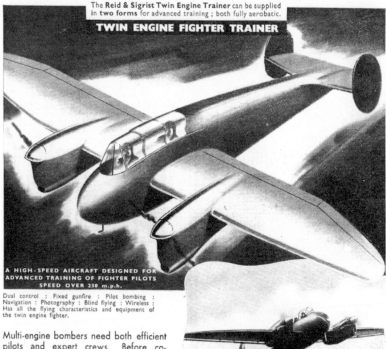

Reid & Sigrist Snargasher

ADVANCED TRAINING

EFFICIENCY in aircraft service necessitates skilled flying instruction in machines designed for this work, with all the characteristics and equipment of the Service types.

The Reid & Sigrist Twin Engine Trainer can be supplied in two forms for advanced training; both fully aerobatic.

TWIN ENGINE FIGHTER TRAINER

A high speed aircraft designed for advanced training of fighter pilots. Dual control : Fixed gunfire : Pilot bombing : Navigation : Photography : Blind flying : Wireless : Has all the flying characteristics and equipment of the twin engine fighter.

Note the Pilot's range of view

TWIN ENGINE BOMBER TRAINER

Multi - engine bombers need both efficient pilots and expert crews. Before co - operation can be effective, airsense in the handling of guns and equipment must have been obtained.

Fitted with retractable undercarriage : Constant speed airscrews : Trailing edge flaps : Balanced rudders and elevator trimmers.

Two 240/260 h.p. engines : Range 650 miles at 200 m.p.h. Overall length 25' 3¾". Detachable wings. Width of centre section 14' 4".

Equipped for advanced training of the bomber pilot and crew. **Supplied with removable Dual Control.** Suitable for defensive gunfire, bombing, photography, long distance navigation, blind flying, wireless and all duties of multi-engine Service aircraft.

REID & SIGRIST LTD.

SHANNON CORNER, KINGSTON BY-PASS, NEW MALDEN

Reid & Sigrist Snargasher

RS.1 Snargasher Technical Data

Dimensions

Span	36ft 4in
Length	25ft 4in
Height	8ft 11in
Wing Area	212 Sq ft

Weights

Empty	3,000lb
Loaded	4,900lb

Performance

Maximum Speed	205mph at sea level
Cruising Speed	190 mph at 75% power at 6000ft
Stalling Speed	65mph
Initial Rate of Climb	1,330ft per minute
Service Ceiling	18,000ft
Absolute Ceiling	20,000ft

Range

Fuel Consumption	21.8 gallons per hour normal duration
Endurance	4 ¼ hours at 190 mph
Range	800 miles

In July 1939 the Snargasher was taken abroad for exhibition at the Second International Salon of Aeronautics in Brussels and although interest was shown and praise high, no orders resulted. It is also important to note that had the Second World War not intervened the RS.1 could well have been seen on the air racing circuit as it was entered in the King's Cup Air Race which was scheduled to take place in Birmingham on 2nd September 1939.

Throughout the Second World War the Snargasher was used by Reid and Sigrist mainly for communications duties, but during 1941 it was utilized by 7 Elementary Flying Training School (EFTS) at Desford in a training experiment. Over a four-month period from March to June, selected pupils were given a full *ab initio* training course; results obtained were quite satisfactory, but this method of training was not adopted. Only the one example of the Snargasher was produced and a projected development of the design of the RS.2 was shelved during the war.

As for the fate of the RS.1 most accounts state that it was written off during 1944. Former employees have said that this was due to a landing accident and the guilty party on the occasion is reputed to have been a Canadian pilot named Gilliver. The company did have hopes that the aircraft might be repaired but the damaged was deemed to be too substantial for repairs to be viable. Much of the Snargasher was then scrapped, but the fuselage was retained for some years.

Reid & Sigrist Snargasher

A spotter's report in the magazine Air-Britain Digest for July 1950 confirms that it was still to be seen gathering dust in a hangar at Desford at the time. On a final note, information from three separate sources indicates that the fuselage was still present when the airfield and buildings were sold in 1953. During clearing up operations it was consigned to a bonfire.

During 1939 Reid and Sigrist moved its aircraft design department from Shannon Corner to Desford; this was primarily in order that it might be on hand to deal with the increasing work associated with military contracts centered at the company airfield. It was from the design office that Reid and Sigrist's second aircraft originated, the Desford Trainer, appearing in completed form during the summer of 1945.

Snargasher Registration Document

The RS.1 G-AEOD as it appeared at the Brussels International Salon in July 1939
(Photo Air Britain Archive via JM Collection)

Chapter Two
The Desford Trainer

Designed by Charles Bower, the Desford Trainer was built in conditions of secrecy at Desford during the closing stages of the Second World War. Once again, the company chose to have major sections of the airframe manufactured away from the airfield. This contract was undertaken by the Austin Veneer Company of London, one of many similar concerns within the furniture industry at this time, which had been pressed into work associated with wooden aircraft. After completion, the wings, fuselage and tail unit came by road to Desford for assembly followed by the installation of engines, flying controls and ancillary equipment.

An interesting story concerns the assembly of the machine which was completed in the former lecture block on the south side of the airfield. The building comprised two rooms one of which housed the design department, the other the experimental workshop. This was an excellent arrangement as work on the project could be easily supervised by the design office and at the same time secrecy maintained.

The workshop had a double door type of emergency exit which was also the only means of access from outside. This door proved to be an adequate way of entry for the large components mentioned above, but when the aircraft was ready to emerge it was a different story. It was a relatively easy matter to remove the fuselage from the wing and detach the tail unit after the flying controls had been disconnected, these components then went readily out through the emergency doors. This was not the case with the wings which was a one piece structure, complete with engines and under-carriage – additions that made it impossible for the wing unit to go out through the doorway in the manner by which it had been brought it. So, two wooden cradles were made to fit around each engine and undercarriage leg, castors were fitted to the cradles which then allowed the whole unit to be maneuvered while still maintaining a horizontal "flying" position.

One night after working hours, efforts began to solve the problem of removal. First the door frame was taken out, then large sections of brickwork were removed. This enlarged hole then enabled the wing unit to be manhandled out. Immediately this had been done the doorway was re-installed, the brickwork restored and then camouflaged. Work continued throughout the night so that by starting time next day everything appeared normal with the aircraft relocated in an out-of-the-way corner of the flight test shed ready for final re-assembly and subsequent test flying.

The aircraft was given the company designation RS.3 and named after its birthplace, Desford. It showed some resemblance to the RS.1 and probably to a greater extent the shelved RS.2 project, but evidence is lacking to prove this. The design concept can be traced back to early in the war from advertisements appearing in Flight magazine. These depict an aircraft of similar layout to the RS.1 but with much finer lines and two-seat tandem accommodation. Although purporting to illustrate the Reid and Sigrist Trainer (the RS.1 Snargasher) to all intents and purposes the aircraft shown is the RS.3 Desford (See photo on next page). The illustration in the advertisement was taken from a photograph of a model which remained in company hands at Braunstone until 1971 when it was presented to Leicester Museums (see photo on page 27) .

Like its predecessor the RS.1, the RS.3 Desford was of wooden construction with fixed cantilever undercarriage. The wing was one piece, two-spar structure bolted to the monocoque fuselage while the all wood strut braced tailplane had twin fins and rudders mounted as end plates. Intended to serve as an *ab initio* and intermediate trainer the crew of two were seated in separate tandem cockpits, the pupil in front, with full blind flying equipment and the instructor at the rear. Both cockpits were enclosed by a one-piece molded sliding canopy which could be jettisoned, the wind screen structure was strengthened to form a crash bar should the aircraft turnover. Registered G-AGOS (see Aircraft history chapter for more detail) the RS.3 flew for the first time on the

The Desford Trainer

9th July 1945, powered by two 130 hp de Havilland Gipsy Major Series I engines. Following the initial flight, the Desford undertook an intensive test programme in which no major problems were reported. Reports indicate that, like its predecessor the Snargasher, it possessed good flying characteristics. When shown to representatives of the aviation press early in 1946 it received excellent reviews being variously described as 'the complete trainer' and 'an instructors aeroplane' (see chapter Early Marketing Campaign). It received a full Certificate of Airworthiness on 30th May 1946 and participated in the Society of British Aviation Companies (SBAC) Show at Radlett. Throughout the late 1940's, a vigorous sales campaign was mounted in an effort to find buyers for the Desford. It participated in several major exhibitions and was a welcome addition to airshows.

An advertisement depicting the Desford trainer design shown in an RAF camouflage paint scheme

The Desford Trainer

Fully aerobatic, its sparkling performance in the hands of company pilot, C F French and J A Hart were often the highlight of the air display. Interest in the basic trainer version was shown by several foreign countries including Argentina, Egypt and Spain. During May 1947 a twelve day visit was made to Spain, with demonstrations being given to government representatives in Madrid.

The need to diversify the RS.3's role and so attract a wider market led to an experiment being carried out to assess its suitability for agricultural crop dusting. For test purposes a R&S designed belly pannier was fitted and although the Desford did fly in this configuration, no records of the trial have been found (see picture on page 38). In 1946 the company had announced that they proposed to develop the RS.4, which was to be a luxury four/five seat private owners version of the RS.3, but due to lack of outside interest these plans were allowed to lapse (See sketch on page 38). Unfortunately, in spite of all efforts made, no customers could be found for any version of the Desford so, like the RS.1, it was destined to be the sole example of its type.

As interest in the aircraft declined it gradually spent more time idle at the company airfield until eventually it was tucked away at the back of the hangar and almost forgotten. Then in May 1949 it gained a new lease of life when it was acquired by the Air Council to be used for experimental purposes, investigating the concept of the prone pilot position. The famous test pilot Eric "Winkle" Brown of the Royal Aircraft Establishment (RAE) was sent to Desford Aerodrome on the 1st June 1948 to evaluate the RS.3. Following a successful evaluation a contract 6/Aircraft/2695/CB.9(a) was placed with Reid & Sigrist to modify the Desford to provide a prone-pilot position in the extreme nose, details of this project are covered in chapter 4 — A New Lease of Life

Desford Trainer photographed at Radlett Aerodrome in a white colour scheme with black cheatlines along the cockpit

The Desford Trainer

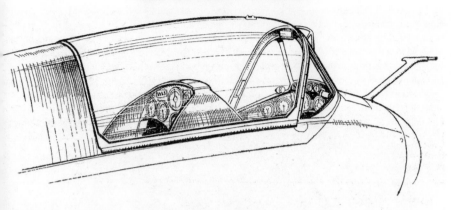

An illustration from an early flight magazine—*"The Reid & Sigrist Desford Trainer has a beautifully formed blown canopy, and the pitot head acts as a horizon datum for pupil pilots"*

A picture of the original concept model built by Reid and Sigrist showing the similarity to the illustration shown on page 25 and the Desford trainer prototype (Leicestershire County Council)

The Desford Trainer

This close up image of the nose shows the large pitot tube and the installation of the Gipsy Major engines with their large drop-down cowlings for ease of maintenance
(Aeroplane via JM Collection)

This front view of the Desford shows that it sits lower than the RS.1 Snargasher although of similar size, the flaps can be seen extended below the centre section
(Aeroplane via JM Collection)

The Desford Trainer

Seen during test flying in late 1945, the Desford demonstrates its large clear-view canopy which would slide back on external rails. The P marking for prototype is painted ahead of the registration and the fuselage roundel is blanked out (Aeroplane via JM Collection)

Visible in this side image are the mass-balance ailerons, strut braced tailplane and the bumper ahead of the tailwheel for rear fuselage protection (Aeroplane via JM Collection)

The Desford Trainer

A photograph showing the Desford Trainer with key personnel involved in the design
Left to Right Dennis Harbin, Stress Calculator, Chas Bower, Design and T. Newton
(Ken Ellis)

(Right) A photograph of the Desford Trainer during a flight near Leicester

The Desford Trainer

9

All who joy would win
Must share it.—Happiness was born a twin.
        Byron—Don Juan.

The Reid and Sigrist Desford (two Gipsy Major motors) (A.F.P. Photo)
ab initio and intermediate trainer in flight near Leicester.

The Desford Trainer

A copy of the original Certificate of Airworthiness application (#7910) for the Desford trainer dated 1945 showing registration details, aircraft classification and basic aircraft dimensions (National Archive Image)

AW/05

AIR REGISTRATION BOARD

12

FULL ~~ABBREVIATED~~ } TECHNICAL CERTIFICATE NO. 92   PROTOTYPE ~~MODIFIED~~

CERTIFICATE OF AIRWORTHINESS APPLICATION NO. 7910

Any certificate of airworthiness for this aircraft should contain those particulars entered in this technical certificate which are numbered to correspond with the numbers in the certificate of airworthiness C.A. Form 59.

FULL NAME, ADDRESS AND NATIONALITY OF OWNER OR OWNING COMPANY

1. Surname of owner, or name of owning company **Reid and Sigrist Ltd.**

2. Christian name

3. Address **Shannon Corner, Kingston-by-Pass**
   Surrey.

4. Nationality **British**

NAME OF CONSTRUCTOR

5. **Reid and Sigrist Ltd.**

NATIONALITY AND REGISTRATION MARKS

6. **G-AGOS**

DESCRIPTION OF AIRCRAFT

Name: **Desford**
7. Type **Trainer.**   Series **1**   Constructor's No **3**

8. Place and year of construction of aircraft **Desford Aerodrome 1945**

Class of Aircraft

9. Land and/or marine **Land**

10. Number of planes **One**

11. Number of engines **Two**

12. Maximum number of persons to be carried (including crew) **Two**

Classification of Aircraft

13. Category **Acrobatic**

14. Subdivision: (a) Public transport for passengers
    (b) Public transport for mails
    (c) Public transport for goods
    (d) Private (e) Aerial work

15. Maximum span (in flying position) **34 feet 0 inches**

16. Maximum length (in flying position) **25 feet 6 inches**

17. Total height (with and without trolley, in the case of marine aircraft) **8 feet 1 inch**

A.R.B. 67

The Desford Trainer

The second page of the original Certificate of Airworthiness application (#7910) showing engine and propeller details. (National Archive Image)

Page No. 2

13

Engines

18. Number installed .... **Two**

19. Makes .... **de Havilland**

20. Types .... **Gipsy Major Series 1**

20a. Engine technical certificate(s) No(s) .... **M.18A** and **18B**

21. International power of the engine(s):

(a) **118/122** H.P. at **2100** R.P.M. at **sea-level** ft. and

(b) ....

22. Fuel consumption at the above-mentioned power, per engine:

(a) **9½** galls. per hour   (b)

23. Oil consumption at the above-mentioned power, per engine:

(a) **1 to 2** pints per hour   (b)

23a. Additional engine data.

Airscrews

24. Number fitted **Two**

Type (a) **2-bladed (wooden** Blade No **Z.3750**

Pitch Range **5.72 feet**   Diameter **6.25 feet**

Type (b)

or any alternative airscrews approved in current Notices to Licensed Aircraft Engineers and to Owners of Civil Aircraft.

33

The Desford Trainer

A copy of the original Certificate of Airworthiness (#7335) for the Desford Trainer showing the place of construction as Desford Aerodrome (National Archive Image)

23 M.C.A. Form 59.

GREAT BRITAIN
AND NORTHERN IRELAND.

Photograph of Aircraft
(*in profile*).

MINISTRY OF
CIVIL AVIATION

CERTIFICATE OF AIRWORTHINESS No. 7335
(*Heavier than air.*)

FIRST PART.

FULL NAME, ADDRESS AND NATIONALITY OF OWNER OR OF OWNING COMPANY.

1. Surname of owner (or name of Company) : Reid and Sigrist Limited
2. Christian name :
3. Address : Braunstone Works, Braunstone, Leicester.
4. Nationality : British.

NAME OF CONSTRUCTOR.

5. Reid and Sigrist Limited

NATIONALITY AND REGISTRATION MARKS.

6. G-AGOS

DESCRIPTION OF AIRCRAFT.

7. Name ' Desford Trainer ' Type — Series I Constructor's No. 3
8. Place and year of construction of aircraft : Desford ,1945.

Class of Aircraft.

9. Land and/or marine : Land
10. Number of planes : One
11. Number of engines : Two
12. Maximum number of persons to be carried (including crew) : Two

Classification of Aircraft.

13. Category : Acrobatic
14. Subdivision : (a) Public transport for passengers
    (b) Public transport for mails
    (c) Public transport for goods
    (d) Private (e) Aerial work

15. Maximum span (in flying position) : 36 feet 0 inches
16. Maximum length (in flying position) : 25 feet 6 inches   Span (wings folded) :
17. Total height (with and without trolley in case of seaplanes) : 8 feet 1 inch

Engines.

18. Number installed : Two
19. Makes : de Havilland
20. Types : Gipsy Major I
21. International power of the engine or engines at { sea level :

118/122 H.P. at 2,100 revolutions per minute and XXXXXXXXXXXXXXXXXX
(International number of revolutions.)

Hourly consumption at sea level at above-mentioned { 22. Fuel : 9½ gallons
power per engine { 23. Oil : 1 to 2 pints   xx

34

The Desford Trainer

The second page of the original Certificate of Airworthiness (#7335) for the Desford Trainer showing propeller information, Aircraft weights, Including MTOW and critical performance and loading data (National Archive Image)

24. **Propellers.**
    Number fitted : ....Two.... Types : ....2-bladed (wooden)....
    Design No. ....2.3750.... Hub No. .... Blade No. ....
    Pitch ....28°.... Diameter ....6.75 feet.... or any of the alternative
    propellers approved in the current Notices to Licensed Aircraft Engineers and to Owners of Civil Aircraft.

25. Weight of aircraft empty, including the liquid in the radiators: ....2463.... lb.
    Weight of fuel and oil (tanks full).

    26. Fuel ....317.... lb.
        (Calculated on a basis of 7.2 lb. per gallon.)

    27. Oil ....49.... lb.
        (Calculated on a basis of 9.0 lb. per gallon.)

28. Weight allowed for operating crew : ....170.... lb.
29. Weight allowed for equipment, excluding wireless apparatus : ....122.... lb.
30. Weight of wireless apparatus : ....Nil.... lb.
31. Maximum commercial load (passengers-goods) authorised when the fuel and oil tanks are full,
    calculated on the weights specified in Items 25–30 : ....183.... lb.
32. Maximum total weight authorised : ....3,300.... lb.

COMPULSORY CONDITIONS.

33. Maximum total weight authorised (write in full). The total weight of the aircraft, including all items of load, is not
    to exceed ....three thousand, three hundred.... lb.
    in the ....category Aerobatic....
    .... lb. in the .... category.
    Except in emergency the aircraft must not be loaded to a weight in excess of .... lb. and a notice to
    .... this effect must be displayed in each pilot's cockpit.

34. Minimum crew necessary : ....One (Pilot)....

35. Inspections and overhauls :
    (a) The aircraft must be examined before flight in accordance with the Orders in Council for the time being in
    force under the Air Navigation Acts, 1920 to 1947.
    (b) The aircraft, each engine and its reduction gear, if any, must undergo overhauls of such nature and at such
    times as may be directed by the authorised aircraft engineer.

36. Stowage : The load must be safely distributed and suitably secured.

37. Distribution of the load. The aircraft must always be so loaded that the centre of gravity position is :
    (a) Within a range of ....33.1.... inches to ....38.3.... inches when the landing gear is extended, and
    (b) Within a range of .... inches to .... inches when the landing gear is retracted.
    forward of the datum point. The datum point is defined as ....28.28 inches forward of the rear
    face of the front spar, measured along the fuselage datum.

38. The number of passengers carried must not, in any circumstances, exceed the number for which seating accommodation
    is provided, except, however, that infants under the age of three years carried in the arms of passengers may be left
    out of account for this purpose.

39. The engine revolutions per minute and the induction boost pressure must not exceed ....2,100....
    and .... except during take-off and in emergency when they must not exceed
    ....2,350.... and .... respectively. A notice to this effect must be displayed
    in each pilot's cockpit.

40. The aircraft must be flown only in accordance with the conditions for flying machines in the normal category laid
    down in the Air Navigation Directions or Regulations for the time being in force before a certificate of the
    aircraft, including all items of load, exceeds .... lb. and the aircraft must not then be flown at air
    speed indicator readings in excess of ....220 miles per hour (191 knots).... A notice
    to this effect must be displayed in each pilot's cockpit.

41. Smoking in the aircraft is not permitted.
    Notices to this effect must be displayed in the aircraft.

42. The landing gear must not be extended when the aircraft is flying at air speed indicator readings in excess of
    .... and the landing gear is fully extended, air speed
    indicator readings of .... must not be exceeded. A notice to
    this effect must be displayed in each pilot's cockpit.

43. The flaps must not be extended at air speed indicator readings in excess of ....110 miles per hour
    (95 knots).... and when flaps are fully extended, air speed indicator readings
    in excess of 110 miles per hour (95 knots) must not be exceeded.
    A notice to this effect must be displayed in each pilot's cockpit.

44. When the automatic pilot is in operation the aircraft must not be flown at air speed indicator readings in excess of
    .... the aircraft controls must not be left unattended.
    A notice to this effect must be displayed in each pilot's cockpit.

The Desford Trainer

The third page of the original Certificate of Airworthiness (#7335) for the Desford Trainer showing sign of the certificate, dated 21st June 1948 (National Archive Image)

3   **25**

PERIODICAL OVERHAULS.

Nature of Repairs	Certificate Valid Date	Result of Overhaul (1)	Date and Place of Overhaul

Important Notice.—The maximum total weight authorised corresponds to the case of the aircraft flying in dry air, at an atmospheric pressure of 760 mm. mercury, and at a temperature of 15° Centigrade. This weight must not in any circumstances be exceeded.

The Minister of Civil Aviation, having regard to the Reports furnished to him, issues the present Certificate of Airworthiness dated *21st June, 1948* in respect of the above-mentioned aircraft in accordance with the Air Navigation Acts, 1920 to 1947, and the Orders in Council in force thereunder.

This Certificate is only valid subject to the above compulsory conditions being fulfilled and until the date shown on page 4 hereof.

D. HALE.

Signed.. Date *21st June, 1948*
by authority of the Minister of Civil Aviation.

SECOND PART.

PRECAUTIONS TO BE TAKEN FOR SAFETY IN NAVIGATION.

/which
A.—Description and position of instruments, equipment and devices with the aircraft must be equipped for navigation and which must be in perfect working order :

Instruments, equipment and devices to be in accordance with the Air Navigation Directions or Regulations for the time being in force.

B.—Equipment essential for preventing or dealing with fire whilst in flight :

Hand fire extinguisher(s) in accordance with the Air Navigation Directions or Regulations for the time being in force.

C.—Equipment essential for rendering first aid in case of accident :

Attention is drawn to the requirement of the Air Navigation Directions and Regulations that the owner of an aircraft, in respect of which a certificate of airworthiness is in force, shall not carry out any modifications which affect the safety of the aircraft without first obtaining the approval of the Minister of Civil Aviation.

The Desford Trainer

The fourth page of the original Certificate of Airworthiness (#7335) for the Desford Trainer showing date of aircraft overhaul taken place on 21st June 1948 (National Archive Image)

4   26

PERIODICAL OVERHAULS.

Date and Place of Overhaul.	Result of Overhaul (1).	Certificate Valid until	Signature of Experts.
21st June, 1948. Desford.	Satisfactory.	20th August, 1948	

(1) The periods of and reasons for suspensions and withdrawals of certificates of airworthiness will in particular be indicated in this column.

NOTES.

No entries or endorsements may be made on this Certificate except in the manner and by the persons authorised for that purpose by the Minister of Civil Aviation.

If this Certificate is lost the Secretary, Ministry of Civil Aviation (A.R.4), should be informed at once, the Certificate No. being quoted.

Any person finding this Certificate should forward it immediately to the Secretary, Ministry of Civil Aviation (A.R.4), Ariel House, Strand, London, W.C.2.

(19839—16156) Wt. 44084—J639 7m in 2 sorts 4/48 T.S. 700

The Desford Trainer

For test purposes a Reid and Sigrist designed belly pannier was fitted and although the Desford flew in this configuration, no records of the trial have been found.

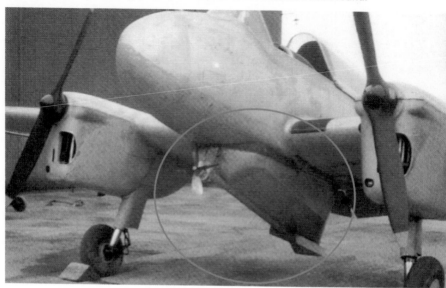

A sketch showing the proposed configuration for the R.S. 4, 4 seater, twin boom aircraft

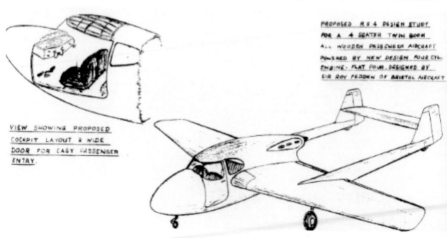

PROPOSED R S 4 DESIGN STUDY
FOR A 4 SEATER TWIN BOOM
ALL WOODEN PASSENGER AIRCRAFT
POWERED BY NEW DESIGN FOUR CYL-
ENGINE - FLAT FOUR. DESIGNED BY
SIR ROY FEDDEN OF BRISTOL AIRCRAFT

VIEW SHOWING PROPOSED
COCKPIT LAYOUT & WIDE
DOOR FOR EASY PASSENGER
ENTRY.

Chapter Three
Early Marketing Campaign

The following chapter includes articles from the aviation press at the time that the Desford trainer was first built and includes reviews from Aeroplane Spotter, Flight, Air Review and Aeroplane. The articles are direct transcripts and provide an interesting and in depth review of the Desford trainer, including flying characteristics and performance. The language used in the articles is very typical of the period, using similes and long sentences to describe the views of the reviewers, rather than the shorter, more technical language that we are accustomed to today.

Some very interesting characters came to put the Desford trainer through its paces including a decorated Second World War Pilot named Wing Commander Maurice A Smith DFC, who went on to become editor of Autocar magazine. You can imagine these experienced pilots turning up and putting the aircraft through aerobatics, including rolls and tight turns before landing and getting in their MG's, smoking a pipe and pondering over what they would write about the Desford.

It seems that the review by Wing Commander Maurice A Smith DFC was a last attempt to try and gain some orders for the Desford, it was now 1948 and no orders were forthcoming. He remarks that:

"It is a great pity in more ways than one that the Reid and Sigrist Desford could not have been ordered as an R.A.F. Trainer"

"On the occasion of my flight, typical Midland weather prevailed. A strong cold wind was blowing; there was full cover of cloud, some showers and indifferent visibility. In addition, I was feeling the after-effects of Deauville. In spite of all this I formed a very favorable impression of the highly maneuverable little Desford which has a character all of its own".

Air Review 1946

"As an economical and versatile training aircraft for the Air Forces of many of the smaller and less affluent nations the Desford seems ideal, and it ought to have a big future in the export market."

The Desford seen during an early test flight

Early Marketing Campaign

Aeroplane 28th December 1945

The Reid and Sigrist Desford

Description and Flight Impressions of a New Twin-engine Two-Seat Trainer

By Flight Lieutenant D.A.S McKay, D.F.M. and Bar

MOST READERS OF THE AEROPLANE will remember the Reid and Sigrist two-motor trainer which appeared early in 1939. Development was held up during the war years, but on July 9, 1945, a second prototype took to the air. Conceived by Sgdn Ldr G.H. Reid D.F.C. and designed by Mr. Charles Bower, chief designer of Reid and Sigrist Ltd, this new aeroplane has for the best few months been undergoing its trials at the firm's aerodrome at Desford, near Leicester.

The Desford trainer is somewhat smaller than the original version and somewhat different in conception. The earlier machine known as the "Snargasher", was designed as a three seat advanced crew trainer, but the Desford is a straight pilot trainer, intended for "all-the-way" training from the ab initio stage to the end of intermediate training. It bears a definite family resemblance to its predessor, but specially noticeable external differences are in the wings, which are now straight tapered instead of elliptical, the vertical tail surfaces, which are now more rounded, and the one-piece sliding cockpit cover. A number of novel and ingenious features are incorporated.

The wings are a one-piece, cantilever, two-spar structure, secured to the fuselage by means of six bolts. The spars are of laminated spruce with plywood webs, with box type ribs and plywood covering with spanwise spruce stiffeners. As on the "Snargasher" , the flaps and ailerons are similar in appearance to the Junkers "double-wing" type found on the Junkers Ju 52 and Ju 87, and are mounted behind the entire trailing-edge of the wings; they extend beneath the fuselage. They are of wood construction, covered with plywood. The ailerons are operated by push-rods, and the flaps by a Theed ram, using suction from the engine induction system. The flaps may be set in any of three positions—neutral, take-off, and approach. An interesting feature is that when the throttle controls are opened with the flaps in the fully down position, the flap lever in the cockpit returns automatically to the take off position (10 degrees). This not only assures maximum lift, but avoids the possibly dangerous loss of height which might be occasioned by raising the flaps too soon after a baulked landing, at the same time doing away with the excessive drag of a fully flapped climb.

The fuselage is an oval-section structure covered with plywood, made up of 21 frames connected by two continuous top longerons, with two bottom longerons broken where the wings are attached to the fuselage. Stringers spaced round parallel to these longerons contribute to the strength of the outer skin, while a horizontal plywood diaphragm runs the whole length of the rear part of the fuselage, to add to its resistance to side loads.

The tail unit resembles the "Snargasher" constructionally, being a cantilever plywood-covered structure with twin fins and rudders mounted at the ends of the tailplane. The rudders and elevators are fabric-covered.

Motor Installation

Power is provided by two 130 h.p. de Havilland Gipsy Major Series I Four-Cylinder inverted In-line motors, driving fixed pitch wooden airscrews and mounted on neat cantilever bearers of Jabroc impregnated wood, supported by both wing spars. The cowling is one of the closest and neatest yet seen on a Gipsy Major, and is in two sections, the lower of which, when removed exposes the whole motor for maintenance purposes. The entire cowling may be removed without

Early Marketing Campaign

disturbing the airscrew. *The cooling air is exhausted under the rear of the nacelles—a welcome change from the rather unsightly "gills" almost universal on Gypsy Major installations. The whole cowling is so close that bulges are necessary to accommodate the engine bearers, but these are more than compensated for by the unusually low frontal area presented.*

Fuel is carried in two Henderson crash-proof tanks, each of 22 gallons capacity, mounted between the main spars, inboard of the motor nacelles. The tanks are mounted on hinged doors in the underside of the wings and can be swung down for inspection.

The undercarriage comprises two fixed semi-cantilever Lockheed airdraulic legs with offset axle and wheel, and the tailwheel assembly is a standard Dowty unit. An auxiliary skid under the rear of the fuselage prevents damage to the fins in the event of the breakage of the tail strut. Dunlop pneumatically operated differential brakes are fitted to the main wheels. The whole airframe is generously provided with inspection doors and a noteworthy point is that all maintenance work may be carried out without entering the cockpit—a point that will be appreciated by ground crews.

The pupil and instructor are accommodated in separate cockpits in tandem, under a single, one-piece, backward-sliding, transparent canopy. Entry to the aeroplane is easy, using the steps below the fuselage, the retractable handhold under the cockpit, and the generous walkways. Handgrips are also provided—one in the partition between the cockpits for the use of the occupants of the rear cockpit, and the other on the top of the windscreen.

Cockpit Layout

The layout of both cockpits is very neat and well though out. The seats are of the bucket type, the rear one being adjustable in flight, designed for use with seat-type parachute and fitted with Sutton harness. In this connection may be mentioned another of the ingenious devices with which the Desford abounds. It is so simple that one wonders why it has not appeared before. This is a small peg on each side of the cockpit on which to hang the Sutton harness straps when the aeroplane is on the ground. This does away with the bugbear of straps carelessly thrown over the side, with resultant damage to the outer covering, and also the mess caused by muddy feet standing on the straps left lying on the floor of the cockpit.

In the front—the pupil's-cockpit, the control column is of dural tube, with half-spade grip, giving the whole rather the appearance of a question mark. As one would expect on the Desford, there is a reason for this, namely, a better view of the compass is obtained than would be the case with the full spade-grip, as any ex-Hurricane pilot will know! The brakes are applied by the usual hand lever in front of the grip, differential action being achieved in the normal manner by the rudder pedals. The rudder pedals are of conventional type, and may be adjusted on the ground through a fore-and-aft range of five inches.

The standard blind flying panel is fitted with, underneath, the two engine speed indicators, on the left the port fuel gauge and oil-pressure gauge, on the right, the corresponding instruments for the starboard motor. The magneto switches are mounted on the top left-hand side of the instrument panel. Full night flying equipment is carried. On the left-hand side of the cockpit is a control box, mounting the two throttle levers. The mixture control levers, formerly fitted on Gypsy Major powered aircraft, have since been removed. Also on this box is the flap selector lever, which, as previously mentioned, is interconnected with the throttle levers, and below it the elevator trimming tab control wheel. To the rear of the box are the two fuel cocks—one for each tank. In the centre of the cockpit, in front of the control column, is a small pedestal carrying a P.8 compass, with, below, the fire-extinguisher selector control. On the right-hand side is the crank for operating the sliding cockpit cover (four and a half turns from shut to fully open), navigation lights, and identification lights switches.

The rear– or instructor's—cockpit is generally similar, but in place of the full blind flying panel.

Early Marketing Campaign

The instruments are limited to airspeed indicator, altimeter, turn and bank indicator, fore-and-aft level and compass. The rest of the equipment in the rear cockpit is similar to, and interconnected with, that in the front cockpit. Incidentally, the difference in the blind flying equipment of the two cockpit suggests a useful way of teaching the pupil to fly by instruments on both the full and limited panel on the same aeroplane.

Starting-up procedure is the same as for any other Gypsy Major powered aeroplane i.e. by hand-swinging with the right-hand magneto switch on contact. When the motor fires, both switches are put on contact. Due to the low thrust line, airscrew swinging is a far easier business than on the average single motor type. A small door in the cowling gives access to the carburetter if necessary. Taxi-ing with two motors and wheel brakes, is very simple, with an excellent view all round, including straight ahead over the nose.

For take-off, the tail trim is wound to about the central position as shown on the pointer alongside the handwheel. The fuel cocks are checked to ensure that they are both on, and the contents noted on the gauges on each side of the dashboard. Flaps are lowered to the take-off position—this is not really essential, except when taking off from very small aerodromes—and the aeroplane is ready to take off.

Flying the Desford

My first impression when, recently, I had the pleasure of flying the Desford, was that there is practically no noticeable tendency to swing on take-off—certainly nothing that cannot be corrected by the merest touch on the rudder. The Desford is well airborne in a matter of a couple of hundred yards, and almost in no time at all the climbing speed of 100m.p.h. is reached. This speed, on full throttle, at a rate of climb of well over 1,000ft. Per minute is maintained. At the desired height, the flaps can be raised; there is very little "sinking feeling" and practically no change of trim.

After the initial period of acclimatization necessary on the new type—a matter of five minutes or so on the Desford – the really magnificent visibility can be appreciated. The impression, in fact, is that of an open aeroplane, without the disadvantage of the chilly winds that blow around one in the average elementary trainer. The controls are delightfully light and very well harmonized, and the general feel is that of a single-motor fighter rather than that of a twin trainer.

As soon as I had reached 2,000ft, I tried the Desford's single motor performance. On either motor this is really something worth experiencing, and only the slightest touch on the rudder is necessary to keep the aeroplane straight. Height is maintained with no difficulty with the "live" motor at its cruising revs of 1,900. Mr. Charles French, the firm's chief test pilot told me that he has had the Desford down to 70 m.p.h., still maintaining height on one motor, without any signs of unpleasant tendencies developing. This is practically the stalling speed of the aeroplane, so the question of single-motor safety speed hardly arises.

The stall in one of the gentlest I have experienced on any aeroplane, and, occurs, with no tendency for a wing to drop, and with only a slight wallowing sensation, at 70 m.p.h. with flaps up, and 62 m.p.h. with flaps in the 30-degree position. The spin is perfectly straightforward, and eight turns, plus recovery, used up just over 3,000ft. Standard recovery procedure is effective in less than one turn.

Aerobatics are a real pleasure in the Desford, although a close watch has to be kept on the engine revs. During any manoeuvre such as a loop which involves a fairly high speed of entry. Due to the exceptional aileron control, a slow roll, commenced at 140 m.p.h., is equally easy. Some form of variable-pitch or constant-speed airscrews would be a help in the higher speed aerobatics, and I understand that these will eventually be fitted.

Early Marketing Campaign

For the approach and landing, speed is reduced to about 100 m.p.h. and the flaps lowered to the approach position. The approach is then made at 80 m.p.h., or rather less if the aeroplane is motored in. The actual landing is simplicity itself, with no tendency to swing after touch-down—provided, of course, that the rudder is not left to its own devices! The wheel brakes are adequately effective and bring the aeroplane to rest in a very short distance.

Taken all round, the Desford shows itself to be a really first-class little aeroplane, with no vices whatsoever. It is a credit to its designer, and, as has been mentioned, incorporates a number of ingenious and novel features, the result of much thought and appreciation of the pilot's point of view. As a trainer, it should cut down considerably both the time and expense necessary to train a pilot up to the advanced stage, although a possible criticism could be levelled at it, in that it may be even too easy to fly. It should also make a useful high-speed communications aeroplane. Certainly, it is an aeroplane in which any pilot, be he ab initio pupil, experienced instructor, or merely someone who wants to get from A to B without wasting time, will feel completely at home, even on his first flight.

REID AND SIGRIST R.S.3 DESFORD
Two-seat primary and intermediate trainer

Dimensions

Span	34 ft
Length	25 ft. 6 ins.
Height	8 ft, 2 ins.
Wing area (gross	186 sq. ft.

Weights

Empty		2,413 lb.
Crew (with Parachutes)		400 lb.
Fuel and Oil		360 lb.
Removable Equipment		65 lb.
Payload		62 lb.
	Total	3,300 lb.

Loadings

Wing	17.75 lb./sq. in.
Power	12.7 lb./h.p.

Powerplant

Two de Havilland Gipsy Major Series I four-cylinder inverted in-line air-cooled motors. Normal output 120 h.p. per motor at 2,100 r.p.m. at sea level. Maximum output 130 h.p. per motor at 2,350 r.p.m.at sea level

Fuel capacity	44 galls.
Oil Capacity	4.6 galls.

Performance

Maximum Speed at Sea Level	162 m.p.h.
Maximum Cruising Speed at sea level	148 m.p.h.
Range at cruising speed in still air	463 miles.
Initial rate of climb	1,100 ft./min.
Service ceiling	17,730 ft.
Absolute ceiling	19,200ft.

Early Marketing Campaign

Photographs which accompanied the previous article

" Aeroplane " photograph

SNARGASHER SUCCESSOR.—The large slotted flaps, ailerons and the fixed undercarriage of the Desford are well shown in the photograph above.

" Aeroplane " photograph

GOOD VISIBILITY.—An indication of the excellent view from the Desford's tandem cockpits may be obtained from this photograph. This prototype bears hybrid markings.

Early Marketing Campaign

Photographs which accompanied the previous article

THE ENGINE.—A view of the port 130 h.p. de Havilland Gipsy Major Series I four-cylinder inverted in-line engine of the Desford. The main-wheel shock-absorbing legs are of Lockheed design.

THE COCKPIT.—The neat layout is noticeable in this view of the pupil's cockpit in the Desford. All the instruments are sensibly grouped around the standard blind-flying panel. The airspeed indicator on the left-hand side is for experimental purposes only.

Early Marketing Campaign

Air Review Magazine Volume 7 Number 5 March – April 1946

Reid and Sigrist's Desford Trainer

By Air Review Staff

We often hear nowadays of a "novelists' novel" or "composers' music" and one feels tempted to describe the new Desford light twin-motor trainer as an "instructors' aeroplane." Not in the sense that it is difficult to fly; so difficult that only a skilled instructor can handle it with safety. On the contrary, it has all the appearance of being one of the safest aeroplanes so far produced. No, we choose this description because the Desford represents the accumulated wisdom of ten years' flying instruction by the Reid and Sigrist organization at their Elementary Flying Training School (EFTS) at Desford Aerodrome, near Leicester. When the Desford was being designed the suggestions of scores of experienced flying instructors as to their ideas of the ideal training aeroplane were taken into account, and in this respect, we believe it is unique.

The name Reid and Sigrist is primarily associated with high-quality aircraft instruments, but it will be recalled that just before the war this firm produced a small twin-motor three-seat trainer known colloquially as the Snargasher. Only one Snargasher was built, and this was used throughout the war at the Desford EFTS on a rather interesting experiment - that of training specially selected RAF pupil pilots solely on the twin-motor type, and comparing the time to go solo with their contemporaries taking the conventional course on Tiger Moths. It was found that the average time on the Snargasher was between eight and fourteen hours, and it was manifest that no additional time was necessary to accustom pupils to twin-motor aircraft. This system, of course, had the noteworthy advantage of cutting out the usual intermediate stage for "twin" pilots, and it seems that the idea will meet with considerable response in the training of civil pilots now that the war is over and economy is the order of the day.

Major [Sqn Ldr] G.H. Reid, DFC, managing director of Reid and Sigrist Ltd, is a staunch advocate of the advantages of twin motor training from the outset and had recently visited South America where he has been "selling" the idea and probably enabling the Desford to assist British export trade at the same time.

An Air Review representative recently had the opportunity of inspecting and flying in the Desford, and formed a very favourable impression. The Desford is a sound practical engineering job, and particular attention has been paid to ease of maintenance and construction. Semi-skilled labour can be employed in the production of the Desford if it is necessary to do so. The two most impressive features of the aeroplane in the air are the excellent performance on one motor and the unrivalled view from the single-piece moulded cockpit hood. The cockpits are well arranged and not too cramped, and the heating system was especially welcome on the day we were flying (a cold January morning). Also demonstrated to good effect in the air was the automatic flap control. The flaps, mounted on extended hinges behind and below the trailing edge, are operated by a vacuum-controlled ram, the suction being supplied by the motor induction system. Neutral, climb, approach and touch-down settings are provided, and the flaps and throttle controls are interconnected in such a way that the flaps are set in the fully down position for landing and if it becomes necessary to make another circuit due to overshooting, the flaps are automatically moved to the 10 degree take-off position as the throttles are opened up. The additional safety afforded by this safety feature is noteworthy, as many accidents have been caused by pupils bringing the flaps too far up when "Going round again" and sinking-in to the ground in consequence.

Early Marketing Campaign

Mention has already been made of the close attention paid to the maintenance problems, and special features of the Desford in this respect include two 22-gallon crash-proof fuel tanks mounted on hinged doors in the under-surface of the wing between the nacelles and the fuselage. This can be swung down clear of the wing for inspection purposes. Both the nose and tail sections of the fuselage are readily detachable for access to flying controls, electrics etc., and the motor cowlings can be released by the removal of five simple fasteners. The complete cowlings can be taken off without disturbing the airscrews. The laminated wooden cantilevered mountings give added accessibility to the motors.

Stressed for a gross weight of 3,300lbs. and of all-wooden construction, the Desford was designed by Mr. Charles Bower to permit full aerobatics and to cover the full curriculum of Royal Air Force flying training. The two-spar cantilever wings are ply-covered and incorporate 5 degrees of dihedral and 3 degrees of positive incidence, there being no twist on the wing. The fuselage is of oval section with plywood covering, and its transverse frames are carried on four main spruce longerons interspersed with light stringers. The twin fins and rudders are also of wooden construction with fabric-covered control surfaces. The twin rudders are operated by cables in the fuselage and push-rods in the tailplane. The elevators are operated by push-rods and the elevator trim tabs by mechanical remote Control.

The power plant consists of two de Havilland Gipsy Major Series I motors fitted with two-blade fixed-pitch wooden airscrews, but a manually-operated variable-pitch airscrew can be fitted as an alternative. At a later stage it is hoped to produce a version of the Desford fitted with Gipsy Major Series 30 motors with constant speed metal airscrews. An interesting feature of the powerplant is a new device by which the revolutions of the two motors are synchronized aurally. This instrument has been produced on principles originally investigated by [Major] Reid.

The fixed undercarriage employs two semi-cantilever Lockheed Airdraulic shock-absorber legs with Dunlop wheels and brakes. Differential braking is obtained in conjunction with rudders when taxying. The tail wheel is of the normal levered suspension type.

The tandem cockpits (pupil in front) are provided with full dual control and blind flying instruments, and the jettisonable sliding canopy is claimed to be capable of withstanding the shock of a crash if the aircraft overturns.

Most flying schools will welcome the fact that the Desford carries enough fuel for a full-days flying without refueling. A combination of moderately low wing-loading (17-181b./sq.ft) and the robustness of the wide-track undercarriage enables the Desford to be satisfactorily flown in all weathers. The manufacturers stress the fact that the Desford us capable of withstanding all rigours of climate, since the glue used throughout the airframe is a synthetic cement which remains unaffected by moisture. The normal range of the Desford, just under 500 miles, can be increased by the addition of an auxiliary belly tank to about 1500 miles, rendering the aircraft particularly suitable for the use of business executives, or as an economical mail carrier.

The clean lines of the Desford are aesthetically satisfying, and are rather reminiscent of the delightful PZL Wyzel (Hound) advanced Trainer produced in Poland before the outbreak of war in 1939.

As an economical and versatile training aircraft for the air forces of many of the smaller and less affluent nations the Desford seems ideal, and it ought to have a big future in the export market.

The RS.3 Desford will be followed by the RS.4, a four-five seat luxury private type with two Gipsy Major 31 motors, in the same category as the new Miles Gemini.

Early Marketing Campaign

In conclusion, brief mention may perhaps be made to the wartime activities of the Reid and Sigrist organization. Apart from operating 5 Elementary Flying Training Schools (EFTS) throughout the country on behalf of the Air Ministry, the Reid and Sigrist factory at Desford Aerodrome employed about 2,000 workers in the production of 700 Boulton Paul Defiant two-Seat fighters, and the repair and modification of lend-lease North American Mitchell bombers for the RAF. A further 1400 employees worked in the firm's instrument factories, the product for which the organization is world famous. The Desford EFTS, the first to be opened by Reid and Sigrist in 1935 under the reserve training scheme, trained no less than 5,000 pilots and navigators between its inauguration and the battle of Britain with only one fatal causality – surely a record !

[*Dihedral angle is the upward angle from horizontal of the wings of a fixed-wing aircraft]

[*Angle of Incidence - On fixed-*wing* aircraft, the angle of *incidence* is the angle between the chord line of the *wing* ... *Wings* are typically mounted at a small *positive* angle of *incidence*, to allow the fuselage to have a low angle with the airflow in cruising flight.]

Specification chart accompanying the article

SPECIFICATION

POWER PLANT
Two D.H. Gypsy Major Series I Four-cylinder air-cooled inverted in-line motors, each with a normal output of 120h.p. at 2,100 r.p.m. and a maximum output of 130 h.p. at 2,350 r.p.m.

TANKAGE
Petrol (Normal) 44 gallons
Oil 4.6 gallons

MAIN DIMENSIONS
Span 34ft 0 in
Length 25ft 6 in
Height 8ft 2 in
Wing Area 186 sq ft

WEIGHTS
Empty (Including standard removable equipment) 2,477 lb.
Crew of two with parachutes 400 lb.
Fuel and Oil 360 lb.
Payload 63 lb.
Loaded Weight 3,300 lb.

PEFORMANCE
Maximum speed at sea level 162 mph
Cruising speed at sea level 148 mph
Range at cruising speed 463 miles
Rate of Climb 1,100 ft/min
Service Ceiling 17,730 ft
Absolute Ceiling 19,200 ft

LOADINGS
Wing 17.75lb/sq.ft
Power 12.7 lb / hp

LATER MODELS
Fitted with two 145 hp Gypsy Series 10 motors with manual v-p airscrews, the top speed is 176 mph and the range 507 miles
Fitted with two 160 hp Gypsy Series 30 motors and constant speed metal airscrews, the top speed is 181 mph and the range 523 miles

---

Early Marketing Campaign

Flight – The Desford Trainer A New- Twin-engined Trainer based on Earlier Reid & Sigrist Design

January 24th 1946

Most pilots freely hand out grouses and, not quite so freely, bouquets to the aircraft which they fly. The flying instructor, however, probably becomes more aware of the good and bad character-istics of his aircraft than anyone and can usually be relied upon to point out this or that which could be altered to the benefit of both instructor and pupil. It is, there-fore, interesting to hear that notice has for once been taken of such criticism and that the recommendations have a material form in a training aircraft. The Reid and Sigrist twin-engined Desford clearly displays a pilot's influence behind design and equipment. At the five Reid and Sigrist flying schools operating during the war, a very large number of RAF pilots received their elementary training. The Desford trainer is in part the outcome of their training experiences. It has been developed from the Snargasher, which was primarily a three-seat trainer for combining elementary and intermediate training in a shortened wartime course. Interesting comparative courses of instruction are understood to have been carried out early in the war, using on the one hand this aircraft and a combined course with pupils picked at random, and on the other, the normal elementary and intermediate types of aircraft and separate standard courses. The successful pupils from the courses were then combined at the operational training stage. The results are not all known, but the combined-course pupils are believed to have shown at least equal skill to the others. The Desford also is intended for the training of pilots from the ab initio stage to the end of the intermediate stage. The idea of the "compete trainer" is that of Sqn Ldr G.H.Reid DFC. Mr Charles Bower, the chief designer of the Reid and Sigrist company, has produced a promising aircraft into which he has incorporated many interesting features.

Basically, the Desford is a low-wing monoplane of wooden construction and, following the modern tendency amongst light aircraft, it has twin fins and rudders. The power is derived from two D.H. Gypsy Major Series I engines, but it is intended that, in due course, the Desford should also be available fitted with either Gipsy Major series 10 or series 30 engines if increased performance is required. These engines were described in the issue of Flight for December 27th, 1945.

The fuselage is a Plywood-covered structure of oval section. Its frames are carried on four spruce longerons, the top two being unbroken throughout the length of the aircraft. These members are interspaced with parallel stringers, and at the rear end there is additional ply stiffening. Small sections of both nose and tail are detachable for inspection purposes.

The two-spar cantilever wings are also of all-wood construction. In plan, they have marked trailing-edge taper, the taper being straight from root to tip. In section, the wing thickness is constant from root to engine nacelle and then tapers evenly to the tip.

"Automatic" Flap Control

An unusual feature of the wing assembly is that the ailerons and flaps are both mounted on extended hinges behind and below the trailing edges. The flaps cover the full available trailing edge and are continued below the fuselage. They are operated by a vacuum-controlled ram, the engine induction system supplying the necessary suction. Four flap settings are provided: neutral, climb, approach and touch-down. Flaps and throttle controls are interconnected in such a way that if the flaps are set in the fully down position, and the throttles are opened (as in the case of an overshoot) the flap control is automatically moved from the down position to the 10 degree take of setting, thus ensuring maximum lift, immediate reduction of drag and avoiding the risk of sinking-in as a result of bringing the flaps too far up. This device is of considerable benefit for training purposes, for which the aircraft is primarily intended, but there is always the risk that,

Early Marketing Campaign

once a pupil has become accustomed to having his flaps looked after for him in an emergency he may well forget that there is no such automatic device on other machines.

The twin fins and rudders are mounted at the extreme ends of the cantilever tail-plane, and like the remainder of the airframe, the tail unit is of ply-covered wooden construction. The control surfaces are wood with fabric covering and are push-rod operated. Two fixed, semi-cantilever Lockheed Airdraulic legs comprise the undercarriage. They are widely spaced and fitted with Dunlop wheels and brakes. Differential braking in conjunction with the rudders is obtained when taxying. The tail wheel is a normal Dowty assembly, but the machine is also provided with a solid tail skid immediately ahead of the tail wheel as an additional safeguard against damage in the event of the tail wheel collapsing in an exceptionally heavy landing.

The four-cylinder, in-line, inverted air-cooled Gipsy Major engines are mounted on laminated wood cantilever bearers, which are anchored to the wing spars. This mounting makes the engines extremely accessible for all general maintenance purposes, and the accessibility is further improved by the neatly detachable engine cowlings. The lower portions of these cowlings are made in one piece and are quickly releasable, each being held in position by five fasteners. The complete cowlings can be removed without disturbing the fixed-pitch wooden airscrews.

A good deal of thought appears to have been given to ease of maintenance on this aircraft. Apart from ease of removal, the cowlings are also provided with three quick release covers, which provide access to the magnetos, fuel pump primers and oil filters. In addition, there are six inspection doors in the fuselage for access to the various controls, including one for the back of the instrument panel, and eight on the wings. Another feature of similar type is that the two twenty-two-gallon fuel tanks are mounted on hinged doors on the under surface of the wing between the engine nacelles and the wing roots. These doors, complete with tanks, can be swung sown clear of the wing for inspection purposes. The general effect of the liberal provision of inspection doors is to ensure that all normal routine servicing can be carried out from outside the machine without entering the cockpits.

Both the nose and the tail sections of the aircraft are easily detachable, the former making access to the rudder bar and accumulator a simple matter, and the latter leaving clear for maintenance the elevator, trimming tabs, rudder controls and the tail wheel oleo.

The tandem cockpits are comfortable, have dual controls and appear to be well laid out. The front cockpit is intended for the pupil and is fitted with a comprehensive set of instruments, including a standard blind-flying panel. Cockpit heating, operated from either seat, is provided on this aircraft and is to be regarded as a necessary luxury on a two-engine training machine. The one-piece sliding hood can be operated from either seat, four and a half turns of the handle being required for the full travel of the hood. Visibility is very good indeed from both seats, and a reassuring feature for the pilot is that the windscreen structure is reckoned to be sufficiently sturdy to bear the weight of the aircraft should it overturn.

The aircraft has been designed to withstand most extremes of climate, and if desired it could be adapted for use as a communication aircraft. A total range up to 1,550 miles can be obtained by fitting an additional faired-in mid-wing, under-belly tank. There is also a scheme for an alternative wider fuselage to seat 4-5 persons, and for providing increased power by fitting Gipsy 30 series engines, so that the aircraft can be used as a small passenger-carrying machine.

———

Early Marketing Campaign

A review of the Desford by a distinguished Second World War pilot on a blustery day to try and rejuvenate interest in the aircraft

Flight – Desford in the air – Renewed Acquaintance with a Popular Basic Trainer Design by Wg Cdr Maurice A.Smith, DFC

July 22nd 1948

It is a great pity in more ways than one that the Reid and Sigrist Desford could not have been ordered as an RAF trainer. Experiments during the war with the prototype three-seat Snargasher, from which it was developed, indicated that interesting results might well have been obtained from the employment of such a twin-engined basic trainer for combined elementary and early advanced instruction. The majority of duties now required of the latest basic trainers such as the Prentice are within the Desford's capacity, although no third seat – a provision of very doubtful value – is available. However, such ruminations are past history, and the Desford in trainer form is remembered as an attractive proposition with some excellent flying characteristics. The existing machine may shortly be employed on important research work which gives added purpose to this appraisal from a pilot's point of view.

One fact worth mentioning at this juncture is that two Gipsy Major engines giving a total of 260 h.p. are cheaper to buy and operate than one 205 h.p. Gipsy Six or 250 h.p. Gipsy Queen 30.

A detailed description of the machine was given in our January 24th, 1946 issue [See previous], but to recall the principal features, it may be mentioned that it has a two-seat tandem cockpit with single bubble – type sliding canopy, and is powered by two close-in Gipsy Major engines. Construction is of wood, landing wheels are fixed, twin fins and rudders are fitted, and the all-up weight is 3,330lb. Provision is made to carry a long-range tank under the belly, and equipment at present includes electrical inter-com, fixed camera in the nose, full blind-flying panels, and a skid indicator for deck landings. In addition, V.H.F. radio can be carried. On the occasion of my flight, typical Midland weather prevailed. A strong cold wind was blowing; there was full cover of cloud, some showers and indifferent visibility. In addition, I was feeling the after-effects of Deauville. In spite of all this I formed a very favorable impression of the highly maneuverable little Desford which has a character all of its own.

The cockpit is snug when the enclosure has been wound forward and the heater turned on. All controls come to hand conveniently, and field of few is first class-as, of course, it should be. Taxying with the differential use of throttles, aided by powerful air-operated brakes with lever on the spade grip, is simple and effortless. Springing is rather hard, and, due to the short fuselage, there was a tendency to buck on the uneven grass surface of Desford airfield. The main legs and wheels are, in fact, a great deal more sturdy than necessary.

For take-off, a few degrees of flap may be selected if desired. Pneumatic operation is employed, and any angle can be selected at will. The flap lever and throttles are interconnected to select automatically the maximum lift position if, with flap down, throttles are opened wide for an over-shoot. Directional control on the ground is very good and, if need be, both throttles can be opened wide at once, rudder being used to check any slight swing tendency. The take-off run, flying solo, was in the region of 150 yards, and initial climb settled down at a good 1,000ft per minute. Coarse-pitch wooden airscrews are fitted at present, and best climbing speed is about 90 m.p.h.

On becoming airborne, the sweetness of aileron control became apparent at once. The aspect ratio is high, and the surfaces are very light and effective in operation, giving an exceptionally

Early Marketing Campaign

good roll performance. They are hinged behind the wing trailing edge in a rather unusual manner. By comparison, rudder and elevator controls, though good, are quite heavy, and those who value harmonization highly might regard this as a slight weakness. Personally, I have no objection on this type of aircraft when all three controls are light even if in varying degree.

Single-engine Performance

Directional control with one engine idling is remarkably good and critical single-engine speed is hardly distinguishable from stalling speed. The Desford will climb slowly on one engine at heights up to about 2,500ft, and it will hold height at 3,000ft. If the dead engine could be stopped, which might be possible in some cases, performance would, of course, be better. Turns can be made readily in either direction with one engine cut. The stall, which occurs at around 53 m.p.h. with flap down, is as gentle as anyone could wish, and only after prolonged straight sink does a wing offer to drop. The flap-up stall commences at about 60 m.p.h. I.A.S. Recovery from a spin, which after one turn becomes smooth and steep, is positive and rapid.

One rather unusual feature, which makes itself felt when trying the stall or on steep turns and certain aerobatic manoeuvres, is a warning shudder at about 15 m.p.h. above the normal stalling speed. If a steep turn is held after this turbulence around the tail is felt, speed can be allowed to drop to a figure at least 10 m.p.h. lower before the true stall occurs. Thus, it is not apparently a normal high-speed stall occasioned by high loading in the manoeuvre. A similar manifestation accompanies the over-the-top portion of a loop.

Aerobatics call for no special remarks. All recognized manoeuvres can be executed with ease, including a climbing roll. Rolls are more comfortable if slightly barreled, and the speed should be about 140 m.p.h. Loops can be made from 150 m.p.h. upwards, and for rolls off, about 165 m.p.h. seems sufficient. Care must be taken to avoid over-revving of engines in the dives. As an aid to straight and level flying, the pitot head is mounted on a long arm on the fuselage nose. It acts as a horizon sight and is most useful as such. Normal cruising speed is around 125 m.p.h. indicated, at 3,000ft. The skid indicator is another potentially useful gadget which, by causing one or other of two red lights to wink at the pilot, indicates occurrence and direction of skid, or, according to the position of an accompanying control, skid in excess of a pre-set number of degrees. When approaching to land, some flap may be lowered at not more than 100 m.p.h. and a good steep final approach can be held at 80-85 m.p.h., a trickle of power and three-quarters to full flap being desirable. The Desford will side-slip well if need be, and this would be a useful characteristic in the unlikely event of a forced landing being necessary with this fixed-wheel twin.

For landing, a gentle round-out brings one easily into three-point attitude, and from that position the pilot has little feel except with regard to direction. When ready, the aircraft gives a small shudder and "plops" firmly down.

As one would expect, an overshoot presents no problem and the automatic part-raising of flap is effective. Slight change of trim occurs with the raising and lowering of flap; up causes nose-down moment, and vice-versa. In its two and a half years of flying the Desford has proved very easy to maintain and its condition is still excellent. The designer, Mr. G Bower, paid particular attention to the servicing aspect of the aircraft, and detachable panels are provided at all appropriate points. For example, there are fourteen inspection covers in all on wings and fuselage for examination of the push-rod control system. The crash-proof fuel tanks are mounted on the hinged doors which give access to their compartments and they may thus be swung open for inspection. Engine cowlings can be removed entirely without disturbing the airscrews, and both nose and tail portions of the fuselage are detachable.

Early Marketing Campaign

Reid and Sigrist test pilot, Mr. J.A. Hart flew the Desford for the accompanying photographs

MAKERS DATA FOR THE REID and SIGRIST DESFORD

Two D.H. Gipsy Major Engines

Span	34ft
Length	25.5ft
Height	8.1ft
Wing Area	186 sq.ft
All-up Weight	3.300lb
Wing Loading	17.75lb/sq ft
Power Loading	12.7 l.b/h.p.
Max. Speed	160 m.p.h.
Cruising Speed	140 m.p.h.
Fuel Capacity	44 Gallons
Range	460 Miles
Climb	1,100ft/min
Service Ceiling	17,700ft

Copies of photos which appeared in the article

Unusual wide-span ailerons, hinged behind the wing trailing edge, give the impression of full-span flaps. Aileron control is particularly light and effective. Note the pick-up points for the long-range belly tank beneath the centre section.

Instruments and controls are grouped in a practical manner around the standard blind flying panel. A skid indicator and camera controls may be seen among the more familiar equipment.

Early Marketing Campaign

Flight Advertisement March 28th, 1946

For complete flying training the

D E S F O R D

sets a new world standard in light aeroplanes

New standards in economy of operation and maintenance are set up by the dual-control Desford trainer now on test for the R.A.F. It is the development of a company which besides its fame as makers of fine flying instruments, has trained many thousands of pilots for the R.A.F. in its own schools — and is always willing to co-operate with you over training problems. The Desford is immensely strong. Further, it can be parked out of doors in all weathers. Two unique features are interconnected flaps and throttle controls, and pneumatic-engine revolution indicators. Every point about training — from the first to the last stage — has been thought out and provided for. Owing to the excellent view which both occupants have, it would also be ideal for police patrols or even as a private machine. Full details on request.

PERFORMANCE : With two D.H. Gipsy Major Series I four-cylinder in-line inverted air-cooled engines of 130 h.p. per engine at sea level.

Maximum speed, sea level	162 m.p.h.
Maximum cruising speed, sea level	148 m.p.h.
Cruising range	463 miles.
Rate of climb	1,100 ft. per min.
Absolute ceiling	19,200 ft.
Service ceiling	17,730 ft.

Reid & Sigrist

REID AND SIGRIST LTD. KIRBY MUXLOE, LEICESTER

Early Marketing Campaign

Flight front cover June 20th, 1946 showing an artists impression of what might have been, a second Desford trainer flying in the background and a third on the ground

Early Marketing Campaign

The Aeroplane front cover from July 1945 showing an artists impression of what might have been. A squadron of Desford trainers on the ramp at an RAF Station while a Desford Trainer with RAF roundels flies overhead

JULY 27, 1945

THE AEROPLANE

EVERY FRIDAY
ONE SHILLING

THE DESFORD TRAINER

Fitted with Gipsy Major Series I Engines and Henderson Safety Fuel Tanks, also embodying all the essentials to cover the whole of "ab initio" and "intermediate" stages of flying training.

Reid & Sigrist Ltd
DESFORD

Early Marketing Campaign

The front cover of Flight and Aircraft Engineer from December 1945 showing an artists impression of the Desford Trainer in flight

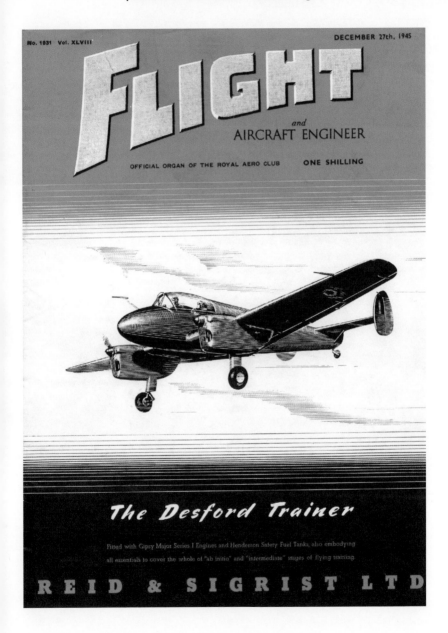

No. 1931 Vol. XLVIII

DECEMBER 27th, 1945

FLIGHT

and AIRCRAFT ENGINEER

OFFICIAL ORGAN OF THE ROYAL AERO CLUB   ONE SHILLING

The Desford Trainer

Fitted with Gipsy Major Series I Engines and Henderson Safety Fuel Tanks, also embodying all essentials to cover the whole of "ab initio" and "intermediate" stages of flying training.

REID & SIGRIST LTD

Early Marketing Campaign

The Aeroplane Spotter December 27, 1945

THE REID AND SIGRIST R.S.3 DESFORD

A PRIMARY AND INTERMMEDIATE TRAINER, the new Reid and Sigrist Desford trainer is a development of the Reid and Sigrist Snargasher which appeared early in 1939. Fitted with two 130 h.p. de Havilland Gipsy Major Series I four-cylinder inverted in-line motors, the Desford trainer bears the works number R.S.3.

The Desford trainer is a two-seat low-wing monoplane fitted with twin fins and rudders and a fixed undercarriage. Covered in plywood, the one-piece wing is of two-spar construction, bolted to the fuselage. Wing flaps and ailerons are set below and behind the trailing edge, similar in principle to the Junkers type "double-wing." Both the oval section fuselage and the tail unit are covered in plywood. A feature of the Desford design is the neat cowlings fitted to the Gypsy Majors, each cowling being divided into two sections, the lower half of which, when removed, leaves the whole motor exposed. This is only one example of the many features incorporated which make maintenance easy on the Desford. A one-piece sliding canopy covers the cockpit, which has two seats arranged in tandem. The front cockpit for the pupil is fully equipped with blind flying Instruments, whereas the instructor's panel has many of these instruments deleted. Two 22-gallon fuel tanks in each wing are fitted to hinging panels which swing down clear of the wings.

As a trainer the Desford fulfils all that is required of such an aeroplane, the important feature being that it can be used for training pilots right through from the ab initio stage to the intermediate stage before they pass on to more advanced types. The first prototype is registered G-AGOS

Dimensions – Span, 34ft. 0 in.; length, 25ft. 6 ins; height, 8ft. 2 ins.; wing area 186 sq. ft.

Weights – Empty, 2,413lb.; loaded 3,300 lb.

Performance – Max. Speed, 162 m.p.h. at sea level; cruising speed, 148 m.p.h.; initial climb 1,100 ft./min.; service ceiling, 17,730 ft.; range, 463 miles.

Early Marketing Campaign

THE REID AND SIGRIST R.S.3 DESFORD

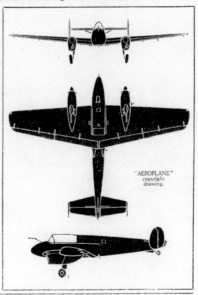

"AEROPLANE" copyright drawing.

A PRIMARY AND INTERMEDIATE TRAINER, the new Reid and Sigrist Desford trainer is a development of the Reid and Sigrist Snargasher which appeared early in 1939. Fitted with two 130 h.p. de Havilland Gipsy Major Series I four-cylinder inverted in-line motors, the Desford trainer bears the works number R.S.3.

The Desford trainer is a two-seat low-wing monoplane fitted with twin fins and rudders and a fixed undercarriage. Covered in plywood, the one-piece wing is of two-spar construction, bolted to the fuselage. Wing flaps and ailerons are set below and behind the trailing edge, similar in principle to the Junkers type "double-wing." Both the oval section fuselage and the tail unit are covered in plywood. A feature of the Desford design is the neat cowlings fitted to the Gipsy Majors, each cowling being divided into two sections, the lower half of which, when removed, leaves the whole motor exposed. This is only one example of the many features incorporated which make maintenance easy on the Desford. A one-piece sliding canopy covers the cockpit, which has two seats arranged in tandem. The front cockpit for the pupil is fully equipped with blind-flying instruments, whereas the instructor's panel has many of these instruments deleted. Two 22-gallon fuel tanks in each wing are fitted to hinging panels which swing down clear of the wings.

As a trainer the Desford fulfils all that is required of such an aeroplane, the important feature being that it can be used for training pilots right through from the ab initio stage to the intermediate stage before they pass on to more advanced types. The first prototype is registered G-AGOS.

DIMENSIONS.—Span, 34 ft. 0 in.; length, 25 ft. 6 ins.; height, 8 ft. 2 ins.; wing area, 186 sq. ft.

WEIGHTS.—Empty, 2,413 lb.; loaded, 3,300 lb.

PERFORMANCE.—Max. speed, 162 m.p.h. at sea level; cruising speed, 148 m.p.h.; initial climb, 1,100 ft./min.; service ceiling, 17,730 ft.; range, 463 miles.

THE SPOTTERS' A.B.C.—CXX

VOUGHT AND VULTEE VARIANTS.—Designated the OS2U by the U.S. Navy, the Vought-Sikorsky Kingfisher is a landplane or seaplane observation monoplane, which has seen service with the Royal Navy. A Pratt and Whitney Wasp Junior R-985-AN-2 drives a two-blade bracket-type airscrew. A single-seat carrier-borne fighter, the Vought-Sikorsky F4U-4 Corsair is powered by a Pratt and Whitney Double Wasp R-2800 radial motor. A commercial version of the XPBS-1, the Vought-Sikorsky VS-44A can carry up to 39 passengers. Motors are four Pratt and Whitney Twin Wasp radials. The Vultee V-1A is an eight-seat transport fitted with a single Wright Cyclone R-1820-G2 radial motor. A fully retractable undercarriage is fitted. Designed as a ground attack bomber, the Vultee V-12A was developed from the Vultee V-11. Power is supplied by one 1,600 h.p. Wright Cyclone GR-2600-A5B motor. First flown in 1939, the Vultee Valiant 51 is a two-seat basic trainer with retractable undercarriage. One 550 h.p. Pratt and Whitney R-1340-53-H1-G air-cooled radial motor is fitted. Basically a (1440 Valiant 51 with fixed undercarriage, the Vultee Valiant 54 exists in two main versions. As the BT-13 it is fitted with a 450 h.p. Pratt and Whitney Wasp Junior R-965-25, and as the BT-15, with a 450 h.p. Wright Whirlwind R-985-AN-1 or AN-3 motor. The Vultee Vanguard 48 is one of a series developed since the outbreak of war, originally intended for Sweden but later diverted to China. As the P-66 of the U.S.A.A.F. it is fitted with a 1,200 h.p. Pratt and Whitney Twin Wasp R-1830-S3C4-G motor. Designed as a dive bomber, the Vultee Vengeance is fitted with a Wright Cyclone GR-2600-A5B-5 radial motor. Considerable numbers have been supplied to the R.A.F. Originally designated the O-59, the Vultee Vigilant high-wing liaison monoplane of the U.S.A.F. is now designated the Vultee L-1. Power is supplied by a 230 h.p. Lycoming R-680-9 radial motor. The Vultee Vigilant Floatplane is fitted with an Edo amphibious float undercarriage.

Chapter Four
A New Lease of Life

Following the purchase of the Desford trainer by the Air Council, the RS.3 remained at Desford where, eventually, a conversion was carried out to enable it to participate in service experiments. The Desford was given the new designation of RS.4 and called the Bobsleigh as the prone pilot sat in the same type of position as you would if on a bobsleigh. Alterations to the aircraft involved a drastic re design of the forward fuselage which resulted in the deletion of the front cockpit, the aft cockpit being provided with a windscreen and sliding canopy. An extended nose section was fitted to house a pilot in the prone position, this resulted in an increase in the total length of the aircraft to 26ft 11in. The new extension was not roomy enough to permit rudder pedals to be fitted so the controls for all three axes were incorporated in a specially designed twin grip control with 3 degrees of freedom.

The modification included dual controls, allowing either of the two pilots (Prone or upright) to control the aircraft, the prone pilot being able to operate all controls by hand. The prone pilot would lie on a ramp to which a safety harness could be attached, the ramp was fitted with two adjustment mechanisms which could be used during flight. The first adjustment mechanism altered the ramp rake through a range of 6.75 degrees, and the second adjustment was used to accommodate pilots between the height of 5ft 6inches and 6ft. Entry to the prone position was via a hinged door in the upper port side of the fuselage, and to the rear position by a sliding hood. Neither the hood or the door could be jettisoned in an emergency. The front end of the fuselage consisted of a one-piece transparent molded nose which acted as a windscreen for the prone pilot. In addition there where two clear vision panels on either side an one in the floor.

An engineering drawing showing the prone pilot flying control system (National archive)

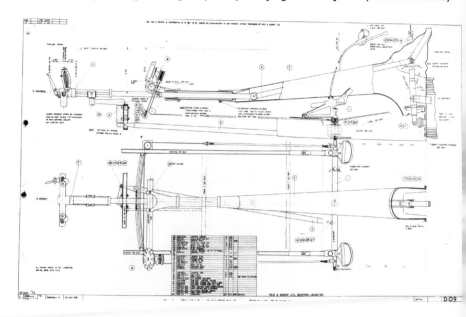

A new Lease of Life

The control column in the rear cockpit was altered to accommodate a fitting for the connection to the prone pilot's controls, and the radio "press-to-transmit" switch was mounted at the top of the handgrip. The rear cockpit rudder bar was also re-designed to suit the modified control system including a new run for the rudder control cable.

The flying controls designed for the prone pilot position could all be manually operated using a flying control box with two handgrips, the three primary flight controls were operated as follows:

Elevator — Fore and aft movement of the control box by means of a push or pull on either or both handgrips

Aileron — Sideways rocking movement of the handgrips by twisting the wrists. Either or both of the handgrips could be used.

Rudder — Sideways movement of the control box by means of pressure applied to either or both of the handgrips.

The left hand grip also incorporated a "press-mute" radio switch and the right handgrip a "press-to-transmit' radio switch.

The flap operations lever worked in a quadrant on the engine control box with the elevator trimmer wheel being mounted on the side of the engine control box, as in the rear cockpit. A rudder spring bias gear was provided with the trimmer wheel being mounted on the main support tube for the ramp, this trimming gear was not duplicated in the rear cockpit. A rudder trim position indicator was fitted on the floor of the aircraft.

An engineering drawing showing plans of the nose extension, the side entry hinged door and side clear vision panels (National Archive)

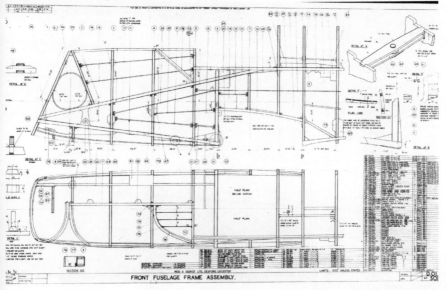

A New Lease of Life

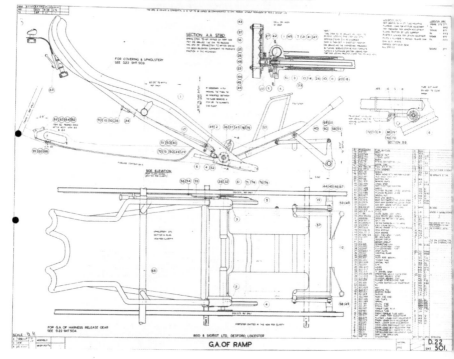

An Engineering drawing showing the adjustable ramp for the prone pilot (National Archive)

A side image of the Bobsleigh showing the one-piece transparent molded nose and side access door

A New Lease of Life

A photograph of Squadron Leader H A Howes testing a mock-up of the prone pilot layout (H A Howes)

A view from the conventionally-seated pilot's cockpit, looking forward to the prone pilot cradle and controls. The rear pilot's rudder pedals and control column can be seen in the foreground (H A Webster)

A new Lease of Life

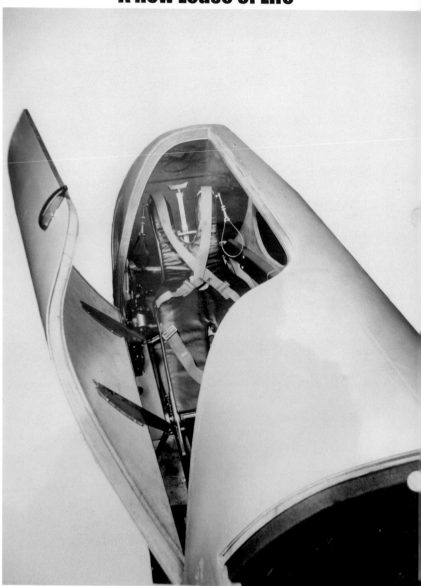

A photograph taken during the conversion of the Desford looking forward towards the nose with the side access door open showing the prone pilot position (Leicestershire County Council)

A new Lease of Life

A closer view with the side door open showing the prone pilot position in more detail as well as the side view windows. (Leicestershire County Council)

A new Lease of Life

A photograph taken during the conversion of the Desford looking forward towards the extended nose before fitting of flight equipment, wiring and instrumentation, the amount of timber lamination can be clearly seen. The wooden construction of the original Desford trainer simplified the conversion of the nose section (Leicestershire County Council)

A new Lease of Life

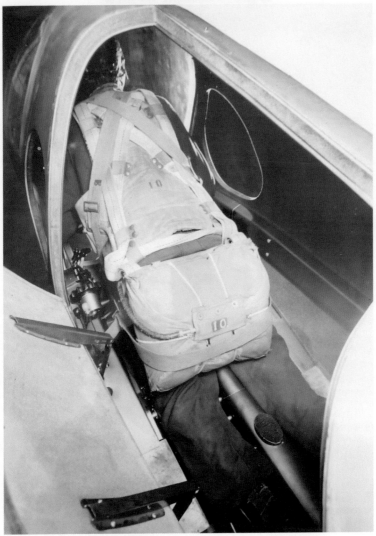

A photograph following conversion showing the pilot in the prone position with parachute attached and side access door open. (Leicestershire County Council)

A New Lease of Life

(Above) A view looking from the front of the Bobsleigh prior to the fitment of the Perspex nose cone, the prone pilots cradle and hand controls can be seen (Below) a view of the prone pilots cradle before installation in the nose of the Bobsleigh. The resemblance of the cradle to a Bobsleigh can be clearly seen (Leicestershire County Council)

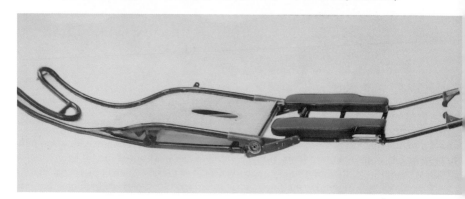

A New Lease of Life

A view of the rear pilots cockpit showing conventional seat, throttle, control column and Instrument panel (Leicestershire County Council). (Below) Later view of the rear instrument panel while in storage

A New Lease of Life

Views showing the lamination of the extended nose (Above and below) and interior views showing throttle and electrical cabling (Next Page)

(Leicestershire County Council)

Auster Aircraft, based in Rearsby were involved in some parts of the conversion, Reid and Sigrist used their expertise in producing the Auster Aircraft to make specialized components like the prone pilot's seat cradle.

A New Lease of Life

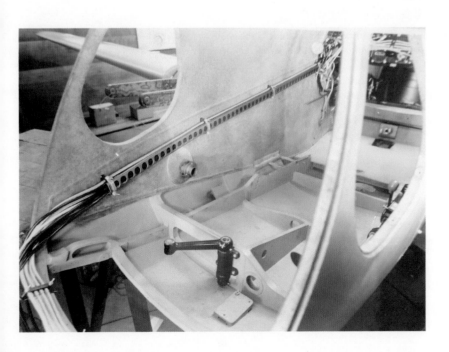

A New Lease of Life

Bobsleigh Prototype Notes detailing the specification of the aircraft

Introduction

1. The Bobsleigh is a twin-engine, low-wing, fully-cantilevered monoplane with ailerons and flaps of the auxiliary aerofoil type, and with a fixed (tail wheel type) undercarriage. It is powered by two Gypsy Major 8 engines, each driving a two-bladed fixed pitch metal propeller. It is designed to permit aerobatics and to cover the curriculum of RAF flying training from a Prone Pilot position.

2. In general the structure is of timber (Birch 3-ply and Grade A Spruce with hard wood where stresses are concentrated).

3. Cellobond Adhesive (which is impervious to moisture) has been used for glued joints.

4. The fuselage is of semi-monocoque construction and is attached to the main planes by four main bolts and two auxiliaries.

5. The main plane is of full cantilever design, all wood, stressed-skin, and two spar construction, It is built in one, the lower surface of which is flush with the underside of the fuselage.

6. Vacuum operated flaps are provided from the centre line of aircraft to 48 degrees of the wing spar.

7. The ailerons are of 20 degrees chord, mass balanced and have an angular range of 13.3 degrees up and 9.9 down.

8. The tailplane is of single spar, all wood construction and is braced to the fuselage by a single strut on either side.

9. The tailplane and bracing struts are readily detachable from the fuselage.

10. The fins are built into the tailplane.

11. The two elevators are connected in way of the fuselage, by a torque tube and are massed balanced. Each consists of a single "D" spar with ribs, covered with doped fabric.

12. The rudders are horn balanced and of similar construction to the elevators, and covered with doped fabric.

13. The landing gear consists of fixed main wheels of 10ft 2 ins (static) track and a fully castoring tail wheel. The main leading wheels are fitted with differential action brakes which are coupled with the rudder bar. The oleo leg radius rod and drag strut fairings are of streamline section and the whole is readily detachable.

14. The rear pilot is seated on the centre-line of the aircraft with provision for a prone pilot immediately in front of him. The rear seat has a 3" adjustment vertically and the ramp for the prone pilot has adjustments (which can be made inflight), first for "Ramp" rake through 6.75 degrees, and also for pilots of statures between 5'6" and 6'.0". Both positions are provided with harness. Entry to the aft position is by a sliding hood, and to the prone position by an hinged door. Neither the hood nor the hinged door are jettisonable. Provision is made for cold air ventilation in both cockpits. The cabin is partially soundproofed by a lining of seapak internal flocking. In the prone position forward, the three controls—Elevators, Rudders, Ailerons—are hand controlled. These controls are coupled to the orthodox system in the rear cockpit.

A new Lease of Life

A view showing the castoring tail wheel design with the rear tail section removed (Leicestershire County Council)

A view (Below) showing starboard undercarriage leg and wheel with front attachments to main plane (Leicestershire County Council)

A New Lease of Life

Engine Upgrade

The modification of the Desford trainer into the RS.4 Bobsleigh also included an engine upgrade where the original Gipsy Major I engines were replaced with more powerful Gipsy Major Series VIII engines fitted with fixed pitch metal propellers. Throttle controls were connected to the control box in the rear cockpit by levers and torque shafts and mechanical remote control was used to connect the control boxes in the front and rear cockpits. Pneumatic engine speed indicators were also replaced by electrically operated indicators, with the generators being mounted aft of the wing front spar and driven by flexible drives which passed through holes in the spar webs to the engine. The starboard engine bay wing front spar was also modified to give adequate clearance for the engine driven generator. A single engine driven vacuum pump on the starboard engine was also replaced by a Rotax B.2A Vacuum pump which was fitted in the normal position on the side of the engine rear cover, on both engines. The engine cowling were modified to accommodate the new installation

An illustration from the Prototype notes showing the Gypsy Major Engine cowlings

Bobsleigh – Engine cowling removal

Next Page

Photos showing engine bearers and attachment castings on spar

A New Lease of Life

A New Lease of Life

The first flight of the RS.4 Bobsleigh, wearing the military serial VZ728 took place on 13th June 1951, with Sqn Ldr A G Bullmore AFC, at the controls. Bullmore's logbook entry for the first flight reads "Initial test—very tail heavy" . Attempts were made to rectify the fault but after being flown the next morning the following comment was recorded, "Tail heavy and sits right wing low". Later that day after further attention another test revealed that while the tail heaviness had been cured the fault affecting the starboard wing was still present. By the time of the next flight on the 21st of June remedial action had been taken resulting in a satisfactory flying attitude being achieved. During July and August test flying continued, including some flights with Sqn Ldr H A Howes occupying the prone position. All passed without incident and on the 23rd of August 1951 the Bobsleigh was flown to the Royal Aircraft Establishment (RAE) based at Farnborough Airfield by Wg Cdr Hobbs.

While at the RAE, the RS.4 was used mainly by the Institute of Aviation Medicine (IAM) in a programme to determine the feasibility of operating the aircraft in the prone flying position. The aircraft also visited a number of other airfields during this period including Baginton Airfield (Coventry) on the 26th of June 1952, probably in connection with the prone pilot Meteor being developed by Armstrong Whitworth. The Bobsleigh also visited Filton on the 15th and 17th of July presumably in connection with the projected Bristol 185 prone-piloted rocket powered fighter. Flights were also made to West Raynham and Bovingdon in August for demonstrations to pilots and senior officers of Fighter Command and the Central Fighter Establishment (CFE).

It is reported that the unconventional method of control made the Bobsleigh somewhat difficult to fly in this mode so flights were always carried out with a Safety Pilot whose name is the one normally shown in the RAE Flight Log. Other pilots known to have flown as "guinea pigs" in the prone position included Wing Commander H Bird-Wilson of the CFE and the famous Fairey Aircraft test pilot, Peter Twiss.

During May 1953 the series of tests were completed, however the Bobsleigh stayed on at Farnborough until the 3rd of March 1955 when it left for the 15 Maintenance Unit at Wroughton in Wiltshire.

DEEFORD (Bobsleigh)
(Prototype)
GIPSY MAJOR
APRIL 1951

A New Lease of Life

Some Famous Pilots who flew the Bobsleigh

Peter Twiss OBE, DSC & Bar—First Person to fly a jet faster than 1000 mph

Eric "Winkle" Brown CBE, DSC, AFC, Hon FRAeS, RN—Holds the world record for the most aircraft carrier deck take-offs and Landings performed

Harold Arthur Bird-Wilson CBE, DSO, DFC & Bar, AFC & Bar—Flew Spitfires and Hurricanes in the Second World War

A New Lease of Life

Front Instrument Panel (Prone Position) —Original Configuration

The front instrument panel of the original Bobsleigh comprised of the following instruments:

	Top-Left Airspeed Indicator MK.1XD			Top-Right Engine RPM	
	Engine Starter buttons	Centre-Left Altitude Indicator MK.1VA	Centre-Right Rate of Climb / Decent Indicator	Oil Pressure Gauges	Power Warning Light
Bottom-Left Magneto Switches 2 Way Screened	Flap Indicator	Fuel Content Gauge Port Tank	Fuel Content Gauge Starboard Tank	Clock	Brake Pressure Gauge

New Lease of Life

Rear Instrument Panel—Original Configuration. The rear instrument panel of the original Bobsleigh comprised of the following instruments:

	Top-Left Airspeed Indicator MK.1XD	Top-Central Artificial Horizon	Top-Right Rate of Climb Indicator	
Top-Left Engine Speed Indicator	Bottom-Left Altitude Indicator MK.1VA	Bottom-Central Direction Indicator	Bottom-Right Turn Indicator Type T.N.300	Top-Right Pitot Heater Switch Navigation Light
Centre-Left Oil Pressure Gauges			Centre-right Voltmeter	Centre–Extreme right Power Failure
Bottom-Left Starter Switches Push Button Type Magneto Switches 2 Way Screened	Bottom-Left Flap Gauge Vacuum Type F4	Bottom-Central Instrument Gauge Vacuum Type F4	Bottom –Right Brake Pressure Gauge	

A New Lease of Life

Why The Conversion was carried out

With increasing experience after the Second World War of turbojet aircraft, particularly fighters, and a wealth of material gained from German Experiments and designs, the "race" was on for ever faster performance. Turbojet or rocket power required particularly smooth aircraft, but the surface area required to accommodate a pilot seated in the conventional up-right position often dictated the depth of the fuselage. The concept of a prone pilot, got around this problem, allowing an aircraft to be designed with a fuselage not much deeper than the height of its jet engine and offering considerably reduced cross-section with the result of less drag and a smaller target and radar signature from head-on. The test carried out with the Bobsleigh paved the way for a more radical assessment of the prone pilot concept. Armstrong Whitworth Aircraft (AWA) were given a contract by the ministry of supply to convert a Meteor twin jet fighter to take a prone cockpit

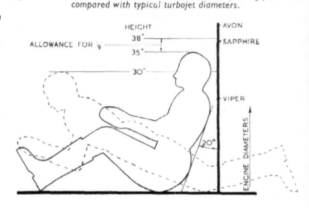

Fig. 1. A "standard man," in conventional and prone piloting positions, compared with typical turbojet diameters.

in the nose. An F8 Version of the Meteor, WK935 was converted and made its first flight from Baginton, Coventry to nearby Bitteswell, on 10th February 1954. The aircraft continued testing the prone pilot concept before being retired. With advancements in aircraft design, including the use of ejector seats in aircraft, the concept of the prone pilot position was not adopted.

As well a developing the prone pilot position to allow for reduced aircraft cross-sections it was also thought that the prone position would reduce the "G" forces experienced by pilots during combat at high speed, but again with the development of equipment like anti G Ttousers and angled crew seats to aid the resistance to G forces, the development of prone pilot positions did not continue.

Meteor prone pilot layout

Following Page

Illustration which accompanied an article in the aviation press describing the attempts at prone-piloted aircraft designs, showing that the Germans had considered ideas during the second World War.

A new Lease of Life

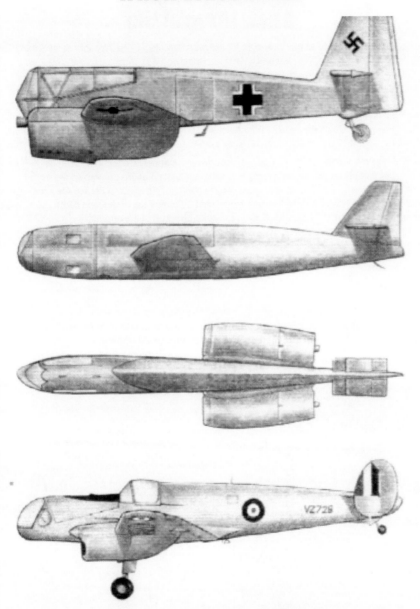

Fig. 2. Three German essays in prone-piloted design, and one British, are illustrated in the author's sketches of (top to bottom) the B.9 research aircraft, DFS 228 reconnaissance sailplane, Gotha P.60 fighter design and Reid and Sigrist R.S.4.

A New Lease of Life

After its period of storage at Farnborough, VZ728 was flown to 15 MU Wroughton on 3rd March 1955 for "spares recovery". However, in 1956 the Bobsleigh was restored by Air Couriers (Transport) Ltd and given the civilian registration G-AGOS and subsequently used as a photographic and survey aircraft, with a camera position in place of the prone-pilot location.
A ferry permit for its flight from Wroughton to Croydon was issued on 16th February 1956 and following conversion, the aircraft received a new civilian Certificate of Airworthiness in January 1958 . The aircraft was then used by Film Aviation Services followed by Kemps Aerial Surveys before being used by a number of private operators (see chapter 5 History for more information).

The following pages (83 –86) are copies of the Ministry of supply Design Certificate showing modification details for prone pilot testing including the pilots that are authorized the fly the aircraft—H.A Howes and A.G. Bullmore as well as aircraft flight limits. A note in the certificate states that the rear cockpit must always be occupied by one of the authorized pilots.
The document is signed by Charles Bower, the chief designer of the aircraft
(National Archive Images)

A photograph of the RS.4 Bobsleigh VZ728 in its prone pilot test scheme when operated by the Institute of Aviation Medicine (IAM) / Royal Aircraft Establishment

DESFORD (Bobsleigh)
(Prototype)
GIPSY MAJOR
APRIL 1951

A new Lease of Life

MINISTRY OF SUPPLY

DESIGN CERTIFICATE
FOR FLIGHT TRIALS OF SERVICE AIRCRAFT

AIRCRAFT _____ BOBSLEIGH

Serial No. ___ 4 ___ Contractor. Reid and Sigrist Ltd,

Spec. No. ___ - ___ Appendix "A" No. ___ C.D. No. 1116

Contract, I.T.P. or Loan Agreement No. M.O.S./6Acft/2695/CB9(a)

Subject of Contract ___ Supply and modification of DESFORD aircraft for Prone Pilot position.

Engine Type ___ Gipsy Major Mk.8 ___ Propeller Type and Drg. No. Fairey A.66904/X1

Recommended blade settings ___ 17° – 48' ___ at ___ 31.2 ___ inches radius.

The above aircraft, represented by the documents listed hereunder, is hereby certified as regards design for the purpose of carrying out:—

    *(i) Flight tests as specified in the attached schedule.

    *(ii) The delivery flight of the aircraft in accordance with the allotment.

    *(iii) Flight by a Service pilot.

Authority is hereby given for these flight tests to proceed with ___ H.A.Howes or A.G.Bullmore or authorised service pilots
as pilot at/from ___ any ___ airfield.

This certificate is only valid when accompanied by a current Certificate of Safety for flight duly signed and dated by the Inspector-in-Charge, A.I.D.

The design of the aircraft is represented by:—

Type Record No. ___ 3 ___ Addenda Nos. ___ 1

and drawings quoted or referred to on the attached list. (See note 9.)

LOADING AND FLIGHT RESTRICTIONS (See Note 1)

(i) MAXIMUM ALL UP WEIGHTS FOR:—
(See notes 2 and 8.)

    (a) Normal take off ___ 3,550 ___ lb.
    (all forms of flying)

    (b) Overload take off ___ - ___ lb.
    (gentle manœuvres)

    (c) Normal landing ___ 3,550 ___ lb.

    (d) Overload landing ___ - ___ lb.

(ii) The aircraft must always be loaded so that the perpendicular projection of the C of G on the datum line falls within the limits defined at (a), (b) and (c) below when the undercarriage is *down*:

A New Lease of Life

Loadings X, Y and Z (See A.P. 970, Chap. 900)		Total Weight (lb.)	C.G. Position		
			~~Aft.~~ ~~Fixed~~ of datum		Aft of datum
(a) Fore and aft limits ... Y ... (at loadings Y & Z)		3,205	30.9 inches		——
	Z	3,279	——	36.3	inches
(b) Full load limits ... ... (range covering all conditions at loading X)		3,550	31.5 inches		——
			——	33.0	inches
(c) Overload limits		–	– inches		——
		–	——	–	inches

(iii) The datum point is 28.28 ins. forward of the rear face of wing front
                      as indicated on Drg. No.D.01/Sheet 501 and is marl
The datum line is by two plates attached to the fuselage external
                      surface on the port side.
The perpendicular distance of the C of G from the horizontal plane containing the datum line

to be within the limits 9.0 inches and 11.0 inches

(iv) The maximum permissible tail ~~XXXXXX~~ wheel load is 510   l
(See note 3.)

(v) The aeroplane has been designed to a flight envelope (AP. 970 chapter 201), defined below
the values quoted being those at which the specified factors are realised at an all up weigh
of 3,550 lbs.
(See note 4.)

Reference point	A	B	B1	C	E	D
ASI (knots)						
EAS (knots)	134.3	282	282	282	–	134.3
n	4.5	4.5	4.5	0	–	2.25

(vi) The following speeds must not be exceeded:
(See notes 5 and 6.)

	Design speed		Speed attained in contractor's flight tests
Maximum speed	191 with fixed pitch propellers	Knots A.S.I.	Knots A.S.I.
Speed flaps down	95	Knots A.S.I.	Knots A.S.I.
Speed undercarriage down	–	Knots A.S.I.	Knots A.S.I.
Maximum Mach. No. ... ... (Indicated)			–

vii) The maximum normal acceleration which must not be exceeded during Trials is 0.9 n1 (+ 0g — ½g) i.e............4.05............g. The maximum normal acceleration attained during contractor's flight tests is..................g at a speed of.....................knots ASI, altitude.........................ft. and all up weight.....................lbs.

viii) Maximum angle of sideslip (AP. 970 ch. 912 para. 7.2).

(a) From design considerations calculations not yet complete, but total $n_v = 0.0624$

| Angle (degrees) ... | (Total n_v for unmodified aircraft = 0.066) |
| Speed (knots ASI) ... ... | Total ℓ_v = -0.054 when C_L = 0.3 |

(b) From contractor's flight tests

| Angle (degrees) ... ... | For the unmodified aircraft, sideslipping in both directions, and with all possible |
| Speed (Knots ASI) ... | flap settings, was satisfactory up to the limit imposed by the use of full rudder. |

(c) Calculated angle of sideslip at which the fin stalls calculations not yet degrees (AP.970, ch. 601, para. 8.3) complete.

(ix) Maximum safe cross wind component at (a) 3,550 lbs and (b) 3,550 lbs. maximum permissible weights:—

  (a) For take off (AP.970, ch. 903, para. 7.3.2.)............15............knots

  (b) For landing (AP.970, ch. 905, para. 7.3.2)............15............knots

(x) (a) The engine limitations quoted in AP   1500B   are to be observed.

  (b) ~~Special engine limitations, which must not be exceeded are~~ ~~(xxxx x)~~

(xi) The pitot and static sources are defined by drg. No. D.15/Sheet 504 Issue A ~~xxxx~~ and D.15/Sheet 505 Issue A.

(xii) ~~xxx~~ *The following } special limitations exist in addition to those specified above and ~~xxx~~ *the following } special precautions are to be taken:—

  (See note 8.)

  The Rear Cockpit must always be occupied by one of the authorised pilots.

Feb. 26th 1953   (Signed)............[signature]............
                        *~~For Principal Director of Technical Development (Airframes)~~
                        *Chief Designer.

•Delete as appropriate.

A New Lease of Life

Note 1.—The scope of the clearance issued for official flight trials must not extend beyond the range of the tests conducted satisfactorily by the contractor. Should values be given other than those obtained by flight test or, in the case of weights and c.g. positions, by direct weighing, comment is to be made accordingly.

The restrictions quoted are derived from the contractor's flight test reports Nos...

....

Note 2.—The maximum all up weight for overload landing is defined as the maximum all up weight at which a landing without structural damage can be anticipated under ideal conditions—i.e. good visibility, no cross wind and a hard and smooth runway. It will normally be near the maximum weight for overload take-off.

Note 3.—In assessing the maximum tail or nose wheel load, consideration is to be given to strength, shock absorbing capacity and shimmy characteristics.

Note 4.—A.S.I. is defined as the instrument reading corrected for instrument error, but not for position error. E.A.S. (equivalent air speed) is defined as the product of the true speed and the square root of the relative density of the standard atmosphere.

Note 5.—If it is necessary to assume a position error to determine the A.S.I. or E.A.S., the best available data should be used. For diving speed limitations, however, the error is to be minus 5 per cent, unless the prior agreement of Structures Dept., R.A.E. has been obtained to a different value.

Note 6.—If a lower speed limitation than that enforced by the Mach. No. quoted under item vi is operative over the lower part of the altitude range, the altitude above which the Mach. No. limitation over-rides the limiting airspeed quoted is to be stated.

Note 7.—If the engine or engine/propeller installation is standard, and no special limitations arise, item x (b) should be deleted.

Note 8.—Any special landing or take-off restrictions necessary (e.g. landing or take-off from a grass surface, deck landing, accelerated take-off) are to be included under item xii.

Note 9.—It is the Chief Designer's responsibility to ensure that the list of drawings defining the aircraft includes any drawing office instructions which have the effect of varying any of the listed drawings in a way which may affect safety.

R.D. (A) Form 13.

Z.2337.R

Chapter Five
Aircraft History

The following chapter details the history and ownership changes of the aircraft from prototype to current status

Owner	Registration	Dates
Reid & Sigrist	G-AGOS	9th July 1945 (First Flight)
	RS.3 Desford Trainer	

Owner	Registration	Dates
Reid & Sigrist	G-AGOS	30th May 1946 (First Airworthiness Certificate issued)
	RS.3 Desford Trainer	

Aircraft History

Owner	Registration	Dates
Air Council	VZ728	25th May 1949 to 17th January 1956
	RS.4	

RAE—Royal Aircraft Establishment

Institute of Aviation Medicine

Converted to Carry out Prone Pilot Position Testing

New Designation:

RS.4 Bobsleigh

Aircraft History

Owner	Registration	Dates
Air Council	VZ728	25th May 1949 to 17th January 1956

Several more views of the RS.4 Bobsleigh whilst operating for the Air Council

Aircraft History

Owner	Registration	Dates
Air Couriers (Transport) Ltd Croydon	G-AGOS RS.4	17th January 1956 to 5th March 1958*

* Re-Engined with 2 x 145HP de Havilland Gypsy Major 10 MK 2 Engines Increasing MTOW

Air-Britain Photographic Images Collection

© Brian Doherty

Letter dated 14th February 1956 showing correspondence between Air Couriers and the Air Registration Board regarding the Permit to Fly

(National Archive)

AIR COURIERS (TRANSPORT) LTD.

CROYDON AIRPORT
SURREY

29

TELEPHONES:
CROydon 8042   CROydon 1748
Ottawick 1313 (night)

Directors:
C. P. L. Godial
F. W. Griffith

AIR CHARTER AND AERIAL PHOTOGRAPHY

Secretary,
Air Registration Board,
Bretterham House,
Lancaster Place,
Strand,
W.C.2.

14th. February 1956.

Dear Sirs,

"Permit To Fly".

We have today applied to M.T.C.A. for a permit to fly the Reid & Sigrist "Desford", G-AGOS from Wroughton to Croydon where we propose carrying out an overhaul for Renewal of the Certificate of Airworthiness.

We will be glad if you will take the necessary action in the matter and we hope the aircraft will be ready to move in about seven days' time.

We enclose our cheque value £2/2/0 .

Yours faithfully,
for Air Couriers (Transport) Ltd.,

Managing Director.

To be treated as an ex-military from point of view of permit. Have told applicant and M.T.C.A.
I have told applicant that the C of A will not be restricted unnecessarily but that it may not be possible to renew it sub-divs other than (d) + (e).

WHILE REASONABLE CARE & PRECAUTIONS ARE TAKEN, THE COMPANY DOES NOT ACCEPT RESPONSIBILITY FOR LOSS OR DAMAGE
TO AIRCRAFT OR OTHER PROPERTY LEFT IN ITS CHARGE.
CUSTOMERS AIRCRAFT ARE FLOWN AND TAXIED AT OWNERS RISK AND RESPONSIBILITY.

Aircraft History

Owner	Registration	Dates
Air Couriers (Transport) Ltd Croydon	G-AGOS RS.4	17th January 1956 to 5th March 1958

Telegrams: "TRANSMINRY, LONDON, TELEX."
Telephone No: MAYFAIR, 9494
EXTN. 2931

28   CA383

MINISTRY OF TRANSPORT
AND CIVIL AVIATION,

BERKELEY SQUARE HOUSE,
LONDON, W.1.

16 February, 1956

Any further communication should be essed to—
THE SECRETARY
and the following reference quoted :—
SG–AD 5252/1/AO91b

Dear Sir,   For the attention of Mr Wheeler

    Aircraft   Desford Trainer, G-AGOS
    Constructor's No.   3

    I should be glad to have the Board's advice as to the issue
of a special permission to fly for the abovementioned aircraft:
the relevant particulars are given below.   If the Board is unable
to recommend the issue of a special permission, will you please
state the reason for considering that permission should be refused.

    Applicant   Air Couriers (Transport) Ltd.,
        Croydon Airport, Surrey.

    Certificate of airworthiness expired on   20th June, 1949

    Proposed flight:
      From   RAF Station, Wroughton
      To   Croydon Airport
      Purpose   Overhaul prior to renewal of certificate of
        airworthiness.

See no reason as
per ex-M.o.S a/c.

        Yours faithfully,

The Secretary,
Air Registration Board,
Brettenham House,
Strand, W.C.2.

DS 84110/1/P2755 800 1/55 DL

Air Couriers Application for permission to fly the aircraft from RAF Wroughton to Croydon

(National Archive)

Aircraft History

Articles appeared at the time providing updates on the aircraft and its move into civilian operations

PRONE TO PHOTOGRAPHY

IN the opening paragraphs of the preceding article mention is made of the first Farnborough venture in prone piloting—the conversion of the Reid and Sigrist Desford trainer by the installation of a special control position in the extreme nose.

By an odd coincidence, as that particular page was going to press, the Desford cropped up again after nothing had been heard of it for several years. It has been acquired from the Air Ministry by Air Couriers, Ltd., who had realized that with its generous "glasshouse" nose and lively performance (something like 166 m.p.h. cruising, 176 m.p.h. top, when Gipsy Major 10s have replaced the two Gipsy Major 1s) it would make a thoroughly useful photographic aeroplane.

Designed and built towards the end of the war by Reid and Sigrist, the instrument firm, the Desford trainer embodied experience which the company had obtained from operating five flying training schools. Towards the end of 1951, the Ministry of Supply released a photograph (*Flight*, November 23rd, 1951) showing the Desford with its new transparent nose, adding the guarded information that it was "being used for experimental flying with a prone-pilot position."

A recent photograph of the Desford at Croydon.

Aircraft History

No Stranger at Filton, where it is seen on the occasion of the recent RAFA Display (news-item on this page), is the Reid & Sigrist Desford, newly restored by the Christchurch Aero Club

Reid and Sigrist Desford

A UNIQUE twin-engined tandem-seater trainer, the Desford, built by Reid and Sigrist, Ltd., of Walton Lodge, Leicestershire, is fully aerobatic. It was found that on the Snargasher, from which the Desford was developed, pupils were able to go solo in from eight to fourteen hours, and it was shown that no additional time was necessary to accustom them to handling larger twin-engined aircraft. Gipsy Major Series 10 or 30 engines are optional to meet particular requirements.

Functions	... ...	Training (various forms)
Construction	... ...	Wood
Power plant	... ...	Two D.H. Gipsy Major Series I
No. of crew	... ...	Two
Span	... ...	34ft
Length	... ...	25ft 6in
Gross wing area	...	186 sq ft
Normal gross weight	...	3,300lb
Normal wing loading	...	18lb/sq ft
Maximum speed	...	162 m.p.h. at sea level
Climb	... ...	1,100ft/min
Service ceiling	...	17,700ft

Aircraft History

Owner	Registration	Dates
Air Couriers (Transport) Ltd Croydon	G-AGOS RS.4	17th January 1956 to 5th March 1958

AIR REGISTRATION BOARD

YOUR REF:
OUR REF: AW/G-AGOS

(Copy to: Mr. R. E. HARDINGHAM)

27

12th December, 19 56.

From L. S. Whicher,

Chancery House.

To The Chief Technical Officer,

Chancery House.

Reid & Sigrist "Desford" Aircraft G-AGOS

Constructor's No. 3

The above aircraft was issued with a Certificate of Airworthiness on the 30th May, 1946 but it appears that it was subsequently taken over by the Royal Air Force and substantially modified. It has now been purchased by Air Couriers Limited at Croydon Airport and an application has been received for the renewal of the original Certificate of Airworthiness.

Further modifications will be carried out by Air Couriers Limited.

In view of the fact that the aircraft has been considerably altered since the Board's original investigation for Certificate of Airworthiness in 1946, Air Couriers Limited have been notified that it will have to be treated as a Prototype (Modified) as there will have to be a certain amount of re-investigation from the design point of view and it will also be necessary to carry out limited flight tests to check the handling characteristics.

The original maximum permissible weight was 3300 lb. and Air Couriers Limited are now asking for 3,550 lb. The 1946 Certificate of Airworthiness was valid in the Acrobatic Category Sub-divisions (a), (b), (c), (d) and (e), and although Air Couriers Limited require the Certificate of Airworthiness renewed to cover the Public Transport Sub-divisions, the firm has been warned that it may only be possible to re-certificate the aircraft under Sub-divisions (d) and (e).

The aircraft is available for inspection at Croydon and clearance will be required by Airworthiness Approval Note.

ADVISE ALL SURVEYORS
ENGAGED ON THIS INVESTIGATION
THAT THE A.A.N. AND/OR T.C. NO IS

4761

INITIALS   DATE 13.12.56

A.R.B. 117
221252

Letters dated 12th December 1956 showing correspondence between Air Couriers and the Air Registration Board discussing proposed changes to the Maximum Take of Weight

(National Archive)

Aircraft History

Owner	Registration	Dates
John Crewsdon	G-AGOS	5th March 1958 to 27th August 1958
Film Aviation Services	RS.4	
(famous Aerial Cameraman and pilot, Killed in helicopter crash in 1983, filmed scenes in James Bond and 633 Squadron)		
RS.4 used for Camera Work		

DESFORD RIDES AGAIN: As described in col. 1, the Reid and Sigrist Desford is now being used for film work. With it in this picture are (left) Mr. Tony Smithson of W. S. Shackleton, Ltd., and Capt. John Crewdson of Film Aviation Services, the new owners.

Film Aspirant

SEEN in the heading illustration is the Reid and Sigrist Desford which, built soon after the war, has been used for a number of experimental purposes, among them investigations of the prone flying position by R.A.E. Farnborough. Following a conversion by Air Couriers, Ltd., who replaced the Gipsy Major Mk 1s with Mk 10s, it has been sold by W. S. Shackleton, Ltd., to Capt. John Crewdson's company, Film Aviation Services. Well known for their helicopter film work, they will use the Desford for special cinematographic duties.

Articles from Flight International

Aircraft History

Owner	Registration	Dates
Air Couriers (Transport) Ltd Croydon	G-AGOS RS.4	1st September 1958 to 30th June 1961
Thomas Hutton Marshall (Ownership Change)	G-AGOS RS.4	4TH July 1961 to 27th July 1962 Restored by Christchurch Aero Club and Appeared at Filton Airshow
John Forbes Nixon (Ownership Change)	G-AGOS RS.4	27th July 1962 to 16th February 1963
Kemps Aerial Services Thruxton (Aerial Camera Work)	G-AGOS RS.4	12th March 1963 to 30th May 1973

Aircraft History

Owner	Registration	Dates
Edward Grace (Restored and painted in non-Standard Camouflage Scheme Appeared a Cranfield Air Pageant in September 1973 (see Log Book Entry on page 100)	G-AGOS RS.4	15th June 1973 to 10th October 1974
Sir William J D Roberts Strathallan Aircraft Collection Perthshire, Scotland Last flight was made in 1978 before becoming a static exhibit	G-AGOS RS.4	11th November 1974 to 8th October 1981 (WFU)
Victor Gauntlet Pace Petroleum Farnham Surrey	G-AGOS RS.4	Ownership Change Purchased at Auction for £5,500 on 14th July 1981 (See Auction Catalogue on page 142)
Scottish Aircraft Collection Trust	G-AGOS RS.4	Ownership Change Donated by Victor Gauntlett

Aircraft History

Owner	Registration	Dates
Leicestershire Museum Service Snibston Discovery Park (Dissembled and stored)	G-AGOS RS.4	1st January 1991 to 1st July 2014

Owner	Registration	Dates
Leicestershire County Council Restored to flying condition by Windmill Aviation	G-AGOS RS.4	July 2014— Present

Aircraft History
Key Log Book Entries

1963—Prone Pilots Seat removed and camera mounting and navigators seat installed in order to carry out aerial survey work

LOG BOOK ENTRY.

Aircraft. Reid Sigrist DESFORD. Registration G-AGOS. Engines. Gipsy Major 10-3

Camera mounting and Navigator's seat, complete with safety harness, installed to Mod. No. .001......... A.A.N. No. 7779....... refers.

Prone pilot's couch and cushion removed.

Seat frame manufactured by R.H.H. Franks, Ltd. Release Note No. C.250.... refers.

Weight Schedule amended and C. of G. position calculated.

I hereby certify that the inspection/overhaul/rep
replacement/modification specified above has be
carried out in accordance with the requiremen
of Chapter A4-3 of the British Civil Airworthin
Requirements. ~~JLButrai~~ LLE.106

3/7/63

Aircraft History
Key Log Book Entries

1973 — Camera equipment removed, military paint scheme and number applied (this was a standard grey green camouflage scheme which the aircraft did not have when in RAF service)

LOG BOOK CERTIFICATE

42

Aircraft Type: Reid & Sigrist Desford Trainer I   Reg: G-AGOS

Engine Type: Gipsy Major 10-1   Serial Nos. Port 10421
                                                Stbd 10151

Propeller Type: Z1510/2/A   Serial Nos. Port 84646
                                                Stbd 84647

)ATE
uly

The following work carried out to theAirframe for Renewal of Certificate of Airworthiness:-

All panels, hatches and fabric patches opened up and internal structure inspected. All glue joints and wood found to be serviceable.
All controls examined and lubricated
Aircraft resprayed to military specification and Registration markings replaced by military number (C.A.A. letter dated 28.6.73. authorises)
New owner's name plate made up and fitted

Instruments

All gyro instruments overhauled by Pandect Limited A/Cert Nos. 065220 and 065 182
Compass check swing carried out

Electrics

Battery removed, examined and recharged
All fuses, bonding and wiring inspected

General

All vertical camera installation equipment removed and equivalent weightfitted in lieu
All minor jobs completed per work sheet attached
Test Flight to Schedule No. 1 completed
All applicable A.D.'s complied with

R Duncan Ltc. 106. 7.7.73 .

Aircraft History
Key Log Book Entries

1976—Worked carried out by Strathallan Air Services for renewal of Certificate of Airworthiness

Strathallan Air Services Ltd.

Tel. Auchterarder 2545   **AUCHTERARDER, PERTHSHIRE**   File Ref. *51/605/1*

LOG BOOK CERTIFICATE

A/c Type: DESFORD   A/c Regn.:   G -AGOS   Constructor's No.

Engine Type.................... S/Nos.   Centre:............................ Port: .... Starboard............................

The following work has been carried out on { AIRCRAFT ~~ENGINE~~ ~~RADIO STN.~~

Work carried out for the renewal of C. of A. @ 767.30 Total A/F. hrs.

50 Hr. Inspection carried out to makers manual.

No Mandatory Mods or insp. applicable to this aircraft.

The requirements of the following C.A.A. Notices satisfied.

20   33   50   55   67

I/We hereby Certify that the Inspection/Overhaul/Repair/Replacement/Modification specified above has been carried out in accordance with the requirements of Chapter A4-3 of British Civil Airworthiness Requirements.

Signed *[signature]*
Authority *[illegible]*
Date *8- 6. 76*

Chapter Six
Bobsleigh-Technical Specification

Prototype Notes

Name:	Bobsleigh
Type:	Twin-engine, low wing landplane
Duty:	Research and development in prone pilot technique
Crew:	Two, Pilot and Co-pilot

Leading Particulars
Principal Dimensions

Complete Aircraft

Length (Fuselage bow to fuselage stern)	26ft 11.75 ins
Span	34ft
Height	
(to top of rudders, tail up)	8ft 9 ins
(to wing tip—tail down)	5ft 5 ins
(to cabin top—tail down)	7ft 9 ins
(to tip of propellers—blade vertical—tail down)	8ft 1 in

Main Plane

Aerofoil Section at root	N.A.C.A.23017 55
Aerofoil Section at tip	N.A.C.A.23012
Chord at Root	6ft 2 ins
Chord at Tip	3ft 1.5 ins
Incidence—to fuselage datum	3 degrees positive
Dihedral—from root	5 degrees positive
Aileron Chord	20% of local wing chord
Trailing edge flap chord	20% of local wing chord

Bobsleigh-Technical Specification

Tail Plane

Span	11ft 0 ins
Chord (Including elevator) at root	4ft 0 ins
Chord (Including elevator) at tip	2ft 0 ins
Incidence	1 deg. 0 min. negative
Dihedral	0 Zero

Rudder

Chord (Max)	1ft 4.7 ins

Fuselage

Length (Frame 1 to Frame 41 See Diagram)	23ft 9 ins
Height (Max with hood closed)	4ft 6 ins
Width (Maximum)	2ft 9.1 ins

Areas

Main Planes, Including ailerons and flaps

Gross	189.6 sq. ft
Nett	168.3 sq. ft
Ailerons, Total	12.7 sq. ft
Flaps (Junker type) Total	18.5 sq. ft

Tail Plane with elevator

Gross	31.93 sq. ft
Nett	30.3 sq. ft
Elevator Total	11.8 sq. ft
Fin and rudder (gross, two, total)	18.32 sq. ft
Nett	18.32 sq. ft
Rudders, two, total	8.52 sq. ft

Bobsleigh—Technical Specification

Fuel System

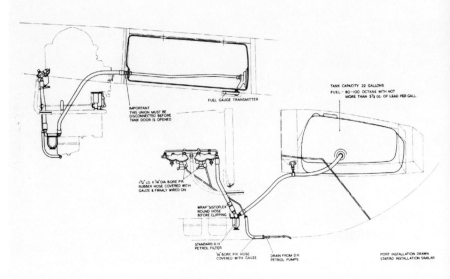

Bobsleigh –Fuel system

Flying Control System

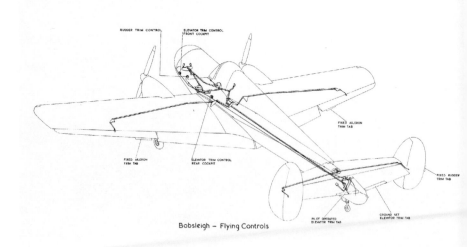

Bobsleigh – Flying Controls

Bobsleigh—Technical Specification

Flap and Vacuum System

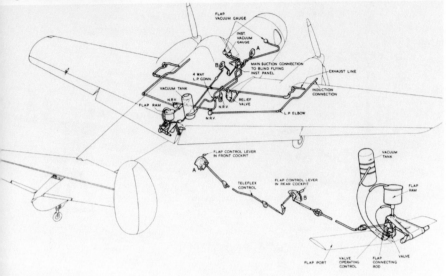

Bobsleigh – Flap and vacuum system

Air Speed Indicator System

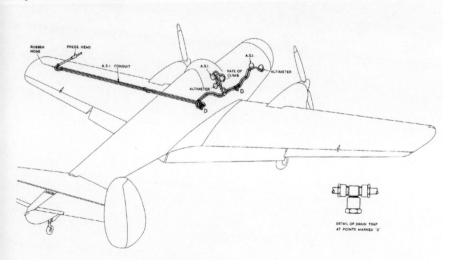

Bobsleigh – A.S.I. system

Bobsleigh—Technical Specification

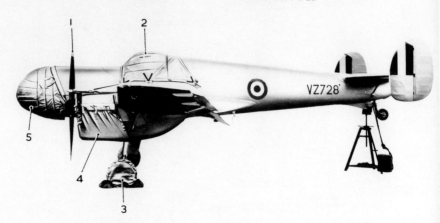

1. PROPELLER ENVELOPES
2. COCKPIT
3. MAIN WHEEL

4. ENGINE
5. PRONE PILOT'S DOME
A PRESSURE HEAD COVER
IS ALSO SUPPLIED

Bobsleigh – Jacking and covers

Bobsleigh—Technical Specification

Original Reid and Sigrist Engineering Drawing illustrating the conversion (National Archive Image)

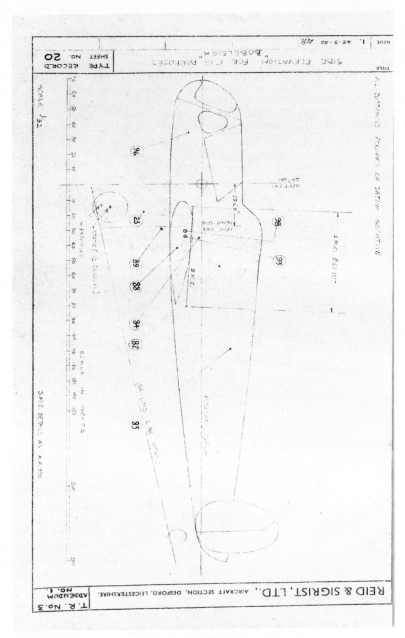

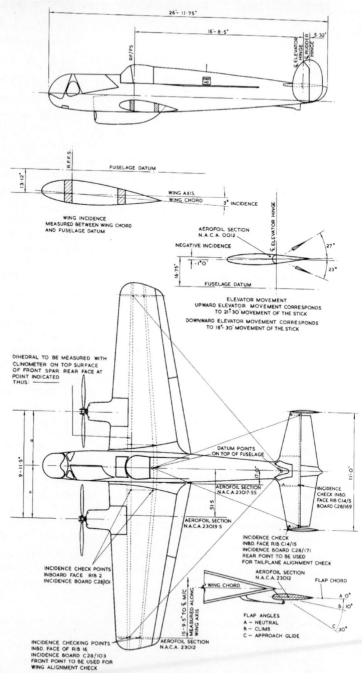

Bobsleigh – Rigging diagram – I

Bobsleigh—Technical Specification

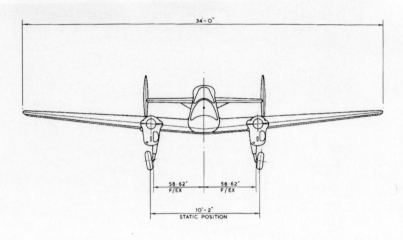

34'-0"

58·62" F/EX   58·62" F/EX

10'-2"
STATIC POSITION

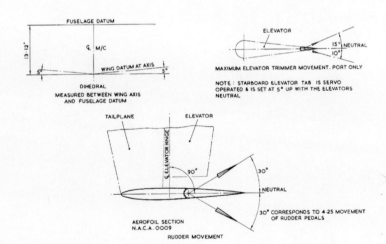

FUSELAGE DATUM

13·12"

C̷ M/C

WING DATUM AT AXIS

5°   5°

DIHEDRAL
MEASURED BETWEEN WING AXIS
AND FUSELAGE DATUM

ELEVATOR

15° NEUTRAL
10°

MAXIMUM ELEVATOR TRIMMER MOVEMENT. PORT ONLY

NOTE : STARBOARD ELEVATOR TAB IS SERVO
OPERATED & IS SET AT 5° UP WITH THE ELEVATORS
NEUTRAL

TAILPLANE   ELEVATOR

C̷ ELEVATOR HINGE

90°   30°
NEUTRAL

30° CORRESPONDS TO 4·25 MOVEMENT
OF RUDDER PEDALS

**AEROFOIL SECTION
N.A.C.A. 0009**

RUDDER MOVEMENT

AEROFOIL SECTION
N.A.C.A. 23012

WING CHORD   13°18'
NEUTRAL
9°54'

AILERON CHORD

AILERON ANGLES

NEUTRAL PARALLEL TO WING CHORD
MAXIMUM MOVEMENT CORRESPONDS
TO 19° MOVEMENT OF STICK

TOLERANCES :–
WING DIAGONALS ± ·50"
TAIL DIAGONALS ± ·25"
MOVEMENTS OF CONTROL SURFACES
RUDDER & ELEVATOR ± $^2_1$° EACH SIDE
ELEVATOR TAB ± $^2_1$°
AILERON { UP) +2°
        (DOWN) −1°
WING INCIDENCE :–
TAILPLANE INCIDENCE ± 15 MIN.
FLAP POS'N { UP) +2°
          (DOWN) −2°

Bobsleigh — Rigging diagram – 2

109

Bobsleigh—Technical Specification

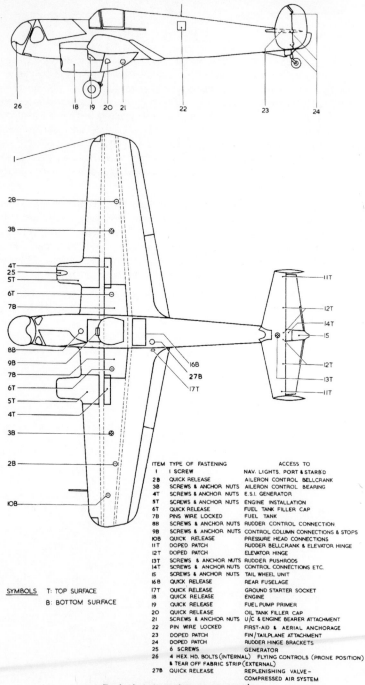

ITEM	TYPE OF FASTENING	ACCESS TO
I	I SCREW	NAV. LIGHTS. PORT & STARB'D
2B	QUICK RELEASE	AILERON CONTROL BELLCRANK
3B	SCREWS & ANCHOR NUTS	AILERON CONTROL BEARING
4T	SCREWS & ANCHOR NUTS	E.S.I. GENERATOR
5T	SCREWS & ANCHOR NUTS	ENGINE INSTALLATION
6T	QUICK RELEASE	FUEL TANK FILLER CAP
7B	PINS WIRE LOCKED	FUEL TANK
8B	SCREWS & ANCHOR NUTS	RUDDER CONTROL CONNECTION
9B	SCREWS & ANCHOR NUTS	CONTROL COLUMN CONNECTIONS & STOPS
IOB	QUICK RELEASE	PRESSURE HEAD CONNECTIONS
IIT	DOPED PATCH	RUDDER BELLCRANK & ELEVATOR HINGE
I2T	DOPED PATCH	ELEVATOR HINGE
I3T	SCREWS & ANCHOR NUTS	RUDDER PUSHRODS
I4T	SCREWS & ANCHOR NUTS	CONTROL CONNECTIONS ETC.
I5	SCREWS & ANCHOR NUTS	TAIL WHEEL UNIT
I6B	QUICK RELEASE	REAR FUSELAGE
I7T	QUICK RELEASE	GROUND STARTER SOCKET
I8	QUICK RELEASE	ENGINE
I9	QUICK RELEASE	FUEL PUMP PRIMER
20	QUICK RELEASE	OIL TANK FILLER CAP
21	SCREWS & ANCHOR NUTS	U/C & ENGINE BEARER ATTACHMENT
22	PIN WIRE LOCKED	FIRST-AID & AERIAL ANCHORAGE
23	DOPED PATCH	FIN/TAILPLANE ATTACHMENT
24	DOPED PATCH	RUDDER HINGE BRACKETS
25	6 SCREWS	GENERATOR
26	4 HEX. HD. BOLTS (INTERNAL) & TEAR OFF FABRIC STRIP (EXTERNAL)	FLYING CONTROLS (PRONE POSITION)
27B	QUICK RELEASE	REPLENISHING VALVE—COMPRESSED AIR SYSTEM

SYMBOLS T: TOP SURFACE
     B: BOTTOM SURFACE

Bobsleigh —Access panels

Bobsleigh—Technical Specification

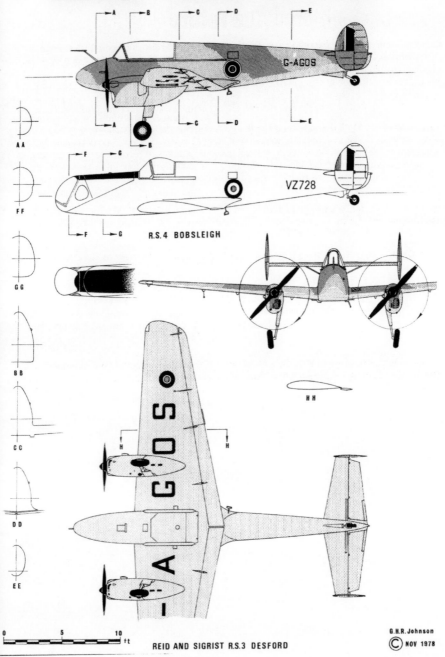

G-AGOS

VZ728

R.S.4 BOBSLEIGH

A A

F F

G G

B B

C C

D D

E E

H H

H

H

REID AND SIGRIST R.S.3 DESFORD

0   5   10 ft

G.H.R. Johnson
© NOV 1978

Chapter Seven
The Future

Currently owned by Leicestershire County council, the Desford was taken out of storage at Snibston discovery park in 2014 and was taken by road to Spanhoe Airfield near Corby, the home of Windmill Aviation. On arrival a full survey was carried out on the aircraft to confirm the condition of the timber structure. Windmill Aviation completed a full restoration of the aircraft, Including overhaul of the engines and propellers, new rubber antivibration mounts had to be specially manufactured. During the restoration work it was found that the Bendix brake system was missing but later located after contacting the Leicestershire Museum Service. In general the airframe was found to be in good condition but there was some work required to replace some of the fabric covering on the main control surfaces like the rudders and flaps as well as the electrical system.

Engine runs and testing followed in 2017 with the aircraft finally taking to the air again on April 22, 2018, nearly 40 years since its last flight in Scotland. Windmill Aviation then conducted 10 hour of flight trials in order to gain a Certificate of Airworthiness for the aircraft. Flight testing was completed on 14th December 2020. Leicestershire County Council's original plan was to offer the aircraft to Newark Air Museum as a static exhibit, but following a petition to keep the aircraft flying, future plans for the aircraft are still under discussion.

The seven year restoration project by Carl Tyers of Windmill Aviation is a fantastic achievement and hopefully the aircraft may be seen flying at airshows in the near future.

The Future

(Above) Photo taken at Spanhoe on 26th August 2017 of the Desford during restoration by Windmill Aviation and (Below) Photo taken at Spanhoe on 10th February 2018

Bibliography

Books

Roy Bonser, Aviation In Leicestershire And Rutland, 2001

A.J. Jackson, British Civil Aircraft Since 1919 Volume 3, 1960

Air Britain Archive December 2011

Magazines

Ken Ellis, Flypast, Lying Down on the Job, March 2019

Roy Bonser, U Bendum, We Mendum, Flypast August 1994

Air Pictorial, Page 272, July 1977

Air Britain Archive, The Reid & Sigrist R.S.3 Desford, Head on View No.40,March 2012

Phil Butler, Air Britain Aeromilitaria, Reid & Sigrist Bobsleigh, Spring 2008

The Aeroplane Spotter , December 27th 1945

The Aeroplane, December 28th, 1945

Flight and Aircraft Engineer , December 27th, 1945

Flight and Aircraft Engineer, January 24th, 1946

Flight and Aircraft Engineer, March 28th, 1946

Flight and Aircraft Engineer , June 20th, 1946

Flight, July 22nd, 1948

Flight, April 4th, 1958

Flight , March 30th, 1956

Flight International, November 8th 1973

Air Review, March-April 1946

Control Column Volume 12, No 8, The Reid & Sigrist Snargasher, November / December 1978

Control Column Volume 13 No 2, The Reid & Sigrist R.S.3 Desford, February / March 1979

Archive Documents

Original Aircraft Logbook (Leicestershire County Council Museum)

National Archive

Websites

G-INFO CAA Registration Website

Flight International Archive

www.edendale.co.uk

www.targeta.co.uk

www.abpic.co.uk

Miscellaneous

David Robinson, Aviation Ancestry

Index

Index

Local interest in the Desford is still very evident— Desford street signs showing an image of the Desford Trainer, and the 'gate guard' at the entrance to the Caterpillar site in Desford

Photo Gallery — Desford Trainer

(Above) Desford Trainer prototype photographed during an early test flight
(Below) Desford Trainer photographed at Radlett Aerodrome (Ken Ellis)

Photo Gallery— Desford Trainer

(Above) Desford Trainer photographed at Rearsby Airfield home of Taylorcraft Auster

(Below) Desford Trainer photographed at Farnborough November 1945

Air-Britain Photographic Images Collection   © george baczkowski collection

Photo Gallery — Prone Pilot Testing

Photos of the Bobsleigh in the RAF colour scheme with registration VZ728

Photo Gallery— Prone Pilot Testing

Photos Gallery — Bobsleigh Civil Operators

(Above) Bristol (Filton) Airshow 1962. Owned by Thomas Hutton Marshall
(Below) Christchurch Airport believed to be 1963

Photos Gallery — Bobsleigh Civil Operators

Air-Britain Photographic Images Collection   © Dave Welch

(Above) Christchurch Airport around 1962/63. Owned by Thomas Hutton Marshall an operated by the Christchurch Aero Club

(Below) Southampton (Eastleigh) Airport believed to be 1963, operated by Kemps Aerial Surveys

Air-Britain Photographic Images Collection   © Dave Welch

Photos Gallery — Bobsleigh Civil Operators

G-AGOS Reid & Sigrist R.S4 Desford Trainer [3]   Alan Lawrence © NA3T

Kemps Aerial Surveys Ltd photographed at Kidlington March 1966

G-AGOS Reid & Sigrist R.S4 Desford Trainer [3]   Alan Lawrence © NA3T

Photos Gallery — Bobsleigh Civil Operators

G-AGOS Reid & Sigrist RS 4 Desford Trainer [3]　　　　　　　　　Barry Hardy col'n © NA3T

Kemps Aerial Surveys Ltd

G-AGOS Reid & Sigrist RS 4 Desford Trainer [3]　　　　　　　　　Brian Stainer (APN) col'n © NA3T

Photos Gallery — Bobsleigh Civil Operators

Operating from Barton Airfield for Kemps Aerial Surveys Ltd

October 25th 1964 (Photos Paul Tomlin)

Photos Gallery — Bobsleigh Civil Operators

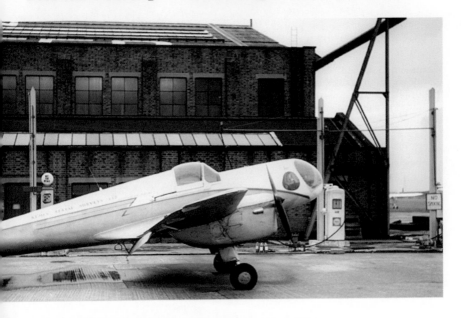

Operating from Barton Airfield for Kemps Aerial Surveys Ltd

October 25th 1964 (Photos Paul Tomlin)

Photos Gallery — Bobsleigh Civil Operators

Operating from Barton Airfield for Kemps Aerials Survey Ltd

October 25th 1964 (Photos Paul Tomlin)

Photos Gallery — Bobsleigh Civil Operators

(Above) Servicing photo and (Below) Photographed at Leicester (Staverton) operated by Kemps Aerial Surveys Ltd

Photos Gallery — Bobsleigh Civil Operators

Photographed at Southampton (Eastleigh) Airfield operated by Kemps Aerial Surveys Ltd

(Below) Seen in camouflaged scheme based at the Strathallan Collection, Scotland

Photos Gallery — Bobsleigh Civil Operators

Photographed at Southampton (Eastleigh) Airfield , July 1965 operated by Kemps Aerial Surveys Ltd (Roy Bonser)

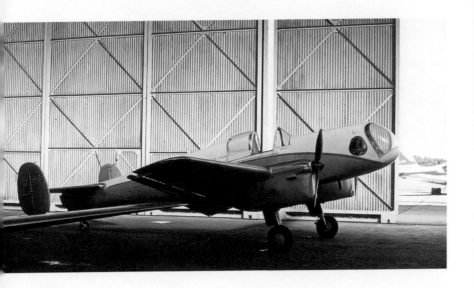

Photo Gallery — Bobsleigh Civil Operators

Reid & Sigrist RS4 Desford Trainer [G-AGOS]

Bill Bushell © NA3T

(Above) Photographed a Cranfield September 1973 and (Below) The Strathallan collection hangar

Photo Gallery— Bobsleigh Civil Operators

Other Views of the Bobsleigh around 1976 at the Strathallan Collection

In storage at Snibston Discovery Park

Photo Gallery— Bobsleigh Civil Operators

In storage at Snibston Discovery Park

Photo Gallery — Recent Restoration

Photographs taken at Windmill Aviation during 2017-2018 restoration (Philip Stevens)

Photo Gallery— Recent Restoration

Photographs taken at Windmill Aviation during 2017-2018 restoration (Philip Stevens)

Photo Gallery — Recent Restoration

Photographs taken at Windmill Aviation during 2017-2018 restoration (Philip Stevens)

Photo Gallery — Recent Restoration

Photographs taken at Windmill Aviation during 2017-2018 restoration (Philip Stevens)

Photo Gallery — Recent Restoration

Photographs taken at Windmill Aviation during 2017-2018 restoration (Philip Stevens)

Photo Gallery — Recent Restoration

Photographs taken at Windmill Aviation during 2017-2018 restoration (Philip Stevens)

ADMISSION BY CATALOGUE ONLY
(ADMITS TWO)

1750-1803
1766
JAMES CHRISTIE
CHRISTIE'S

THE STRATHALLAN COLLECTION
OF HISTORIC AIRCRAFT

TUESDAY 14 JULY 1981
at 2.30 p.m. precisely

The Strathallan Collection of Historic Aircraft

which will be sold at Auction by

CHRISTIE'S SOUTH KENSINGTON LTD.

85 Old Brompton Road, London, SW7 3JS

L. G. M. Hannen (Chairman), W. F. Brooks, F.S.V.A. (Managing Director)
C. J. Elwes, J. W. Collingridge, F.G.A., D. H. Collins, A. Frazer

at Strathallan, Auchterarder, Perthshire, Scotland

On Tuesday 14 July 1981
at 2.30 p.m. precisely

ON VIEW: 11, 12 and 13 JULY FROM 10.00 a.m. to 6.00 p.m.
AND ON THE DAY OF SALE FROM 10.00 a.m. to 2.00 p.m.

ON DAYS OF VIEW AND SALE TELEPHONE, AUCHTERARDER (076 46) 3711 3718

ADMISSION BY CATALOGUE ONLY
Admits two)

In sending Commissions or making enquiries, this sale should be referred to as
STRATHALLAN

The Strathallan Collection Auction

The Desford (Bobsleigh) appeared as Lot 85 in the auction

[85]

85 Ⓐ

1945 REID AND SIGRIST RS3/4 DESFORD (BOBSLEIGH)

G-AGOS/VZ728 Constructors no: 3

Engine nos: 10151 (Port), 10421 (Starboard)

Engines: Two 145 H.P. De Havilland Gipsy Major 10 Mk 2

Wingspan: 34 feet, overall length 26 feet 9in.

All up weight 3,300 lbs.

Engine hours: Port 730.40 since complete overhaul; Starboard 641.45 since complete overhaul.

The RS1 (first prototype) Snargasher was built in 1938 as a twin engined light trainer of all wood construction and was first flown the following year. The RS3 Desford was a development of this aircraft built at Desford, Leicester, equipped with 130 H.P. Gipsy Major I engines. In this form, the machine first flew in July 1945 as G-AGOS. Originally designed as a tandem two-seat, twin engine conversion trainer, the RS3 was evaluated but not ordered by the R.A.F. and was therefore passed to the Ministry of Supply in 1949.

Modified for experimental purposes, the aircraft was fitted with a lengthened glazed nose and provided with controls for prone pilot position flight tests. Re-designated RS4 Bobsleigh (as VZ728), it took to the air in June 1951.

After the completion of these experiments in 1956, the aeroplane was sold back into civilian hands, re-engined with Gipsy Major 10's and used for aerial photographic and survey work until 1974 when it was acquired by the Collection.

Last flown in 1978 and with a total of 775 hours recorded, it is believed to be generally in good condition. The aircraft will, nonetheless, require some attention particularly to the engines.

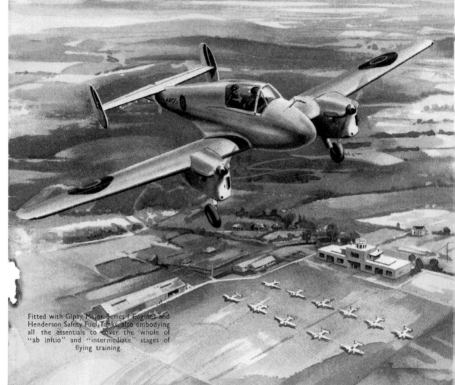

Printed in Poland
by Amazon Fulfillment
Poland Sp. z o.o., Wrocław

91337684R00083